MW00625004

WHEN DEPRESSION AND ANXIETY HAVE A VOICE

WHEN DEPRESSION AND ANXIETY HAVE A VOICE

TANESHIA JOHNSON

TJSelfcare Publishing
Concord, CA

WHEN DEPRESSION AND ANXIETY HAVE A VOICE

This publication is designed to educate and provide general information regarding the subject matter based on the author's experiences. It is published with the understanding that neither the author nor the publisher is engaged in rendering professional counseling services. Each situation is different, and the advice should be tailored to particular circumstances.

WHEN DEPRESSION AND ANXIETY HAVE A VOICE

Copyright © 2019 Taneshia Johnson

All rights reserved. No part of this book may be reproduced in any form or by any electronic or mechanical means including information storage and retrieval systems without permission in written form from the publisher, except by a reviewer, who may quote brief passages in a review.

ISBN-13: 978-0-578-61828-9

Published by TJSelfcare Publishing
Concord, CA

Printed in the United States of America
First Edition 2019

Design: Make Your Mark Publishing Solutions
Editing: Make Your Mark Publishing Solutions

ACKNOWLEDGEMENTS

First, I acknowledge God for His vision that guided me to write this book and His love that He shows me daily. I want to thank my parents for being the vessels God chose to portal me through to this life. I have learned valuable lessons from both of you. Thank you, Mom, for going above and beyond to raise me. I know there were times you wanted to give up, but I thank you for trusting God and believing in yourself.

I thank *all* my family members for your love and direction. I want to thank my grandmother Fannie, who loved me just as my mother did from my birth. My great aunt Rosa for loving me, watching over me, and helping my mother raise me. Thank you to my grandmother Delores. Thank you, Aunt Thelma and Cousin Cynthia for showing the example of what confidence and dedication look like. Thank you to my sister Ife, Aunt Deadra, Uncle Wendell, my step-mother Betty, cousins Carolyn, Kimberly Jones, Kisha Morrow, Gregory Johnson, Anthony Proctor, Marcel Morrow, Lateesha Proctor, Gabrielle Johnson, and Tiara Proctor-Anty, who encouraged me to share my story without shame or guilt. My aunt Geraldine Wilson, thank you for sharing with me the power of God's love, and thank you for loving me and being there when I needed you.

Your vulnerability encouraged me to be vulnerable and open to learning about myself.

My mentor, Ms. Briana Moore, AKA Ms. B, thank you for always keeping it real! For loving me and helping me understand what I was experiencing and how to heal. You show me what it looks like to process feelings and look beautiful while doing it.

Tinisch Hollins, Lashawn Miggins, and Ousha Reed, thank you for giving me guidance and love and embarking on my healing journey with me. You all have played the roles of sisters to me. Watching you all persevere through life with acceptance and peace has shown me I can do the same. I admire how you make necessary changes in your life when needed with courage. You keep me mindful of what I have accomplished in life, and I love you for it. You were there during the hard times. Ousha, you stopped me from losing my mind on many days. When life got hard, we prayed together and helped each other to keep going. Lashawn, you weren't afraid to tell me the truth when I needed it, and you still aren't. You never let me leave your presence without encouraging me. Tinisch, I love you. When I didn't even know who I was or the level of dysfunction I was living, you were there by my side to remind me of the queen that lived inside me.

Thank you to all my friends. I love you and thank you for loving me and supporting me. The following friends have been with me since this book was just a vision in my mind: Deanna Miller, who has loved me since we were age five and accepted me for who I am throughout my entire life. Deanna, you give me courage to keep going, and you remind me of where I have been. Bobby Phillips, thank you for being you. Your friendship has inspired me to find myself and what makes me happy. I may be the only child, but you are the brother I always wanted. Brianna Green, you keep me focused on my goals and always help me laugh through my pain.

Javette Lawrence and Aunt Sherry Lawrence, thank you for encouraging me to keep writing when I wanted to quit and helping me see the diamond inside of me. Javette, you have truly been a blessing. I know God sent you to me. Your beauty is inside and out. I thank you for the nights we prayed together and helped lift each other up with laughs. Love you, girl. Patrice Johnson, thank you for your kind spirit and being my resting place when I feel overwhelmed. Nicole Melton, thank you for your love and guidance. You have helped me stay focused when I got discouraged. Carlina Williams, thank you for inspiring me and motivating me to invest in my dreams. Aresha, thank you for your transparency, support, and love.

Thank you to my graduate school friends: Lazandra, Angie, Nichelle, Ronnie, Alexis, and Toya. All of you played a major role in helping me stay on track in school and with life goals. I appreciate and love you all in ways that would take a lifetime to write.

Zaire Earby, you saw a light in me that I didn't even see in myself. You loved me and pushed me to share my story with the world. Thank you, Cornelius Collins. Cornelius, you were a listening ear and support when I needed you. Alexis Cobbins, thank you for believing in me and encouraging me to put myself and my dreams first. Thank you to my work family. I love you all.

Sankofa is a word in the Twi language of Ghana that translates to "go back and get it." It is visually expressed as a bird that flies forward while looking backward with an egg that symbolizes the future in or near its mouth. I look at my life as similar to this. Therapy helped me understand my past and take the lessons from it I needed to create the life I live now. Thank you to my past therapist as well as my present therapist, who helped me put the pieces of life together and evolve into the person God wants me to be.

And last but not least, thank you to my amazing editor and self-publishing consultant, Ms. Monique D. Mensah. Monique, I have learned what stepping out on faith looks like from you. Thank you for starting Make Your Mark Publishing Solutions and working effortlessly with me. Through my father's death and other life challenges, you continued to encourage me and stay on top of me to finish my book. You truly did turn my manuscript into a masterpiece.

DEDICATION

To my mother, thank you for your sacrifice, love, and guidance.

&

To my dad, thank you for your love,
sense of humor, and support.

SOMETHING IS WRONG

I had just turned thirty, and I hadn't been feeling like myself for a few months. My life was not the life I thought I would have at thirty years old. When I was sixteen, I wrote in my diary that by thirty, I would have three children, a husband, a house with a picket fence, and maybe a dog. Instead, I was single, living with my mother, up to my knees in debt, and had a job I hated.

I was considering therapy. I needed someone to talk to about how I felt. I'd been working as a social worker for eleven years and encouraged my clients to talk to therapists when they needed additional insight on life and emotional support. I was scared to death by the idea that I was a counselor who was contemplating therapy. I was in the process of completing my master's degree in social work and later aspired to do clinical social work, so this felt like defeat. Diagnoses and interventions were still new to me; after all, I was still a student and not yet working with clients in a therapeutic way. However, I could no longer turn a blind eye to what was happening in my life, and I wasn't going to allow it to ruin my future.

It was hard for me to make decisions on my own without other people's input. I was always worried that I was making the wrong decision and the outcome would be a disaster. I decided to call my friend Joanne and see what she thought. Joanne had recently broken up with her boyfriend and found peace at a support group at her church. Every week, she called me and went on and on about what she was learning. She was the only friend I had who was doing a lot of self-work, so she seemed like the right person to talk to.

"Hey, girl. What are you doing?" I said with hesitance in my voice.

"Girl, nothing, watching *Love & Hip Hop.* This show is a mess, and I'm addicted to it." We both laughed. "So, what's up with you?" she asked.

I took a deep breath. "Girl, so I've decided to go to a therapist."

I heard clapping on the other end. "Yes, honey, yes! Do it, Taneshia. I'm telling you, this group has helped me so much. Girl, me and you are both codependents. We both don't know how to quit. We help people until we're exhausted, give people our money and time, even when we don't have it, and we feel like we have to take care of everyone else. Who takes care of us? I probably should be looking into a therapist, too."

I held the phone somewhat confused and worried. Why did she feel I was codependent just because she was, and what exactly did that mean? "Girl, you keep saying that word. Don't try to diagnose me. And what is 'codependent' anyway?" I said, trying unsuccessfully to hide my anger.

"First off, I need you to calm down, Taneshia, because you know I love you. Secondly, codependency is not a death sentence."

"Okay, but you still didn't answer my question. What is it?"

"Ugh, okay, you really need to go to a meeting with me to find out, but a codependent is someone who enables people around them. She takes on everyone else's problems as her own and walks around fixing everybody except herself. Now tell me that's not you or me. Boom!" she said with confidence.

I loved and admired that Joanne was stepping out of her comfort zone. I saw myself in her. She was right, both her and I overextended ourselves way too much, but I didn't feel like it was out of hand. I'm a sweet and empathetic person. I viewed it as a gift and a curse.

I went to bed that night feeling good about speaking to a friend, but I concluded that I was fine and put the idea of going to therapy on the back burner of my mind.

The next day, I got up and got ready for work. Going to work had become a task within itself. On average, it took me fifteen minutes to decide if I was going and another twenty minutes to get out of bed. Most days, I ran late. However, this morning, I was running behind worse than usual.

I heard my mom from the other room. "Taneshia! Get out of that bed!" This was her daily routine, and she was likely tired of it.

"Okay, I'm up," I whined.

"I don't hear the shower!" she yelled back.

I could always count on her. I hopped into the shower, did my hair, threw on some clothes, and got into the car.

It was a beautiful day. The sun was slowly rising, and I could

3

hear the birds chirping as I started the car. As I drove, my cell phone rang. It was my dad.

"Is this my beautiful daughter, Taneshia Johnson?" he said with pride.

"Yes, Dad, it is," I said, laughing.

"This is your dad checking in on you. You headed to work yet?"

"Yes, sir. I am in the car."

"Alrighty. Well, I love you, and I'll call you a little later."

"Okay, Dad. Love you, too. Bye." I smiled and looked for a CD to play. I found one of my Mary J. Blige CDs and put it into the CD player. As the music came on, I started dancing. I forgot about the idea of looking for a therapist and all that crazy talk with Joanne the previous night. I was fine, life was good, and maybe I was just experiencing a few bad days.

I parked my car in the garage at my job and walked up the stairs. Suddenly, I had a thought: *I don't know why you're taking your time; you know you're ten minutes late. Hurry up and get to your desk!*

I ran up the stairs as if someone were chasing me. I passed all my coworkers, throwing up my hand as they waved me down. I had no time to stop and talk.

I got to my cubicle and signed in for work. I took a breath. "Thank God," I said out loud to myself. I signed in ten minutes late, but if they only knew what I was going through, they would commend me for coming in at all.

"Taneshia, you finally decided to join us," a voice said from behind the door. I knew that voice well. It was my supervisor. He had his own office but always found a reason to sit inside mine every morning.

"Good morning, David. How are you?" I said, rolling my eyes.

"I'm fine, but the question is how are you? You're late."

"Yeah, I had some trouble at home this morning. I apologize for not calling. I knew I would be less than fifteen minutes late, so I figured no need to call." The policy in our handbook stated if an employee was less than fifteen minutes late, they weren't required to notify their supervisor, but with a controlling supervisor like David, this policy seemed nonexistent.

He looked at me. "Taneshia, you need to get this together. You've been late for the last month or so. I would hate to have to write you up for this. You're a good employee, but don't think that will save you from getting written up." He gave me an evil glare as he walked out of my office.

I sat at my desk and looked out the window, gazing at people walking on the street, wishing I was one of them. I didn't like the work I did anymore and wanted a change, but I felt stuck because this was the only job that would allow me to leave early twice a week to go to school. I didn't like that my supervisor felt he could say whatever he wanted to me in any tone he wished. I should've told him that, but because I didn't feel like I had a voice, I allowed him to say whatever he wanted while harboring visions of throwing him against the wall.

My thoughts chastised me. *You did it again, Taneshia. Why didn't you say anything? You are a grown woman, not a little girl. Stand up for yourself! Tell him what's happening. Maybe you can take a leave of absence or something. You never do anything you need to do for yourself.*

I heard my work phone ringing. I looked over and saw it was my coworker calling. "What does he want?" I said aloud to myself. I put a smile on my face and answered the phone. "Good morning. How are you doing?"

I heard loud music as he cursed out other drivers while honking his horn. "Shut up! Shut up! I need to get in this lane! Hey, Taneshia. I can't do this traffic this morning. How did you make it already?" he asked.

"My mom woke me up, praise God. Sadly, that still didn't prevent David from threatening me about being late," I said, feeling down on myself.

"Girl, you didn't call him again? Just call and tell him you'll be late. I did."

"Yeah, it won't make a difference. David is just an asshole, period."

"Damn, somebody woke up mad today. Well, I was wondering if you can do me a favor." His voice was low and meek as he prepared to ask.

Say no. You barely made it to work yourself, and your first client is coming in an hour. Take this time to chill. "Sure, what is it?"

"Thank you, Taneshia! You are awesome. I have a client that's coming into the office in twenty minutes, but I'm running late. Can you help her for me?"

My coworker was never available when I needed him, and I was still processing the threat David had just given me. "Okay," I said. "See you when you get here."

I hung up and gazed out the window with a deep sigh. I was disappointed that I hadn't said no.

You have got to be kidding me! This man doesn't ever help you when you need it. You think by helping him, he will help you? Girl, bye!

I was checking my email and beginning to prepare for the day when my cell phone rang. It was my cousin. "Hey, what's up, cuz? How you doing?" I said.

"Hey, cuz. I'm so-so." I heard the sadness in his voice.

"What's the matter?"

"I don't have enough money to pay my light bill this month. Can you help me? I know I still owe you a hundred dollars, but I really need the help. My daughter needed some new shoes bad, and I had to pay rent and other bills."

As I listened to him, I recalled times when he'd asked me for money before using the same excuses, but I loved him and wanted to help. It felt selfish for me to have money and not help my family and friends. "Okay, I'll send it to you today. I've got to go. My coworker's client is here already." I hung up with tears in my eyes. I had lied to him, but I couldn't stand talking to him anymore after he asked me for money—again.

How did I get here?

That morning, I was in my car grooving to Mary J. Blige's album, talking to my parents, feeling good, and now I felt like a train wreck. I looked at the clock. I had about thirty minutes before my coworker's client arrived. "Maybe I *should* look into seeing a therapist."

I thought about it, but I still wasn't ready to admit I needed to see a therapist, so I let the thought pass.

I went through the rest of the work day crying off and on until it was time to go home.

I went to bible class that night and told one of the members about my day. Geneva was so sweet to me. She was like my aunt. I knew she could help me make sense of things. As I shared with her about my coworker and cousin using me, she hugged me tightly and said, "Taneshia, we have to pray and ask God to help us break these codependent chains."

Oh, my goodness! I thought. *There's that word again.* "You are the second person to say that word to me this week," I said.

"Taneshia, I have realized I am codependent, and you might be, too. I really want to start a group for us here at the church. I've been reading about a program curriculum we might be able to use. First, we would need to find other people in the church who might be interested, then we would have to get trained. I'm going to a group this week. Do you wanna come with me and check it out?"

"Okay."

"Taneshia, I can hear the hesitation in your voice. You don't have to if you don't want to. That is part of the self-care codependents need, learning to say no without guilt."

Geneva was using a lot of language I didn't really understand. I figured, like Joanne, she had been brainwashed into thinking we were bad people. I wasn't going to let her or Joanne make me feel like I was codependent, a people pleaser, or any other words they tried to use to label me. I acknowledged that I was a giver and I could use some practice in learning how to say no, but there was nothing wrong with me. Everybody was like that. No one was perfect. Couldn't we all use some finetuning in one area of our lives? Learning to say no was the area I needed to address but without all those labels and terms being projected onto me.

"Yes, I really want to go and learn more about it and see if it could be a benefit to our church," I said.

"Yay! Okay, the meeting is coming up tomorrow," Geneva said, giving me a hug with a smile.

"Okay, see you then." I smiled back and walked out of the church headed to my car.

I knew I wasn't codependent. I was only going to the meeting to support Geneva and prove to Joanne that I had gone to a meeting and found out I wasn't crazy.

The following day after work, I grabbed my bags and headed out the door. I was known for being late to everything. I was always late because I never wanted to go anywhere. I didn't know how to convey to people that my mood was funky and I didn't feel like myself because I didn't know what I was struggling with. I hadn't even admitted to myself yet that I was having a hard time keeping up with life, so I endured people's comments about my tardiness. I generally laughed it off, but this time, something inside me told me I didn't want to be late because of the blessing I might receive once I got there.

I drove up to the church a little nervous and scared. Joanne and Geneva were some of the vessels God used to give me strength in times of wariness. When things were hard, they both said encouraging words to help me gain clarity and stay focused. I knew they meant well, so I was doing this for them.

I looked in my rearview mirror, combed my hair, and put on some lipstick. As I started gathering my purse to leave the car, I had a thought: *You are not codependent. You are here because you're going to learn how to facilitate support groups at your church and finally shut Joanne up.*

"Yes!" I said aloud. "I am *not* codependent." I felt empowered and relieved.

As I entered the church, I looked around for Geneva. Even with all my effort, I was still late, and a speaker was already on stage. I saw Geneva, but there were no seats next to her. I felt someone embrace my shoulder. It was an older woman wearing gloves. I assumed she was an usher.

"Hi, honey. Let me help you find a seat," she said.

"Okay, but please, not in the front. I'm already embarrassed to be late," I said, hoping she'd heard me because I had to whisper.

"Here you are, dear. Be blessed," she said as she directed me to a seat in the second row despite my request.

I felt embarrassed because I was late. I began to think coming was a bad idea. I didn't care about what people thought of me. I knew who I was. I was an amazing person who loved and maybe gave a little too much.

I gave my attention to the speaker of the night. Her story sounded familiar. She described being involved in relationships with men who abused her, cheated on her, and used her for financial support. Tears streamed down her face as she shared how she had spent ten years of her life married to a man who was emotionally unavailable to her and often made her feel that nothing she did was enough. She recalled stories of her childhood when her father was not present in her life, and she explained that her relationship with her father mirrored her relationship with her husband.

I looked around the room, still shocked I was in that space. However, it surprisingly gave my soul comfort and peace. I felt tears coming down my own face. Questions rushed into my head. Were Geneva and Joanne right about me being codependent? After all, they knew my life story and knew more about codependency than I did. I felt confused and scared about what this meant for me. I suspected that my inability to set boundaries in life was causing more problems for me, but I didn't know how to live any differently.

I felt my heart beating, and my palms began to sweat. The woman next to me hugged me and gave me a tissue. I felt a familiar pain. I had been experiencing sharp pains in my chest for a while but didn't know the cause. I kept telling myself I should go to the doctor, but I didn't have the time.

She whispered, "It's okay to cry here."

I was coming to the realization that codependency may be a part of my identity.

As the speaker ended, everyone clapped. A man came on stage and gave her a hug. "Praise the Lord. Isn't that amazing? The power of God can help us move mountains, you all. Let's have a word of prayer. Please bow your heads," he said.

As I bowed my head and folded my hands to pray, I looked to the left and right. Everyone seemed sincere. I could feel that they were ready to change their lives and, most importantly, I felt the presence of God in the building. The woman next to me was crying. I didn't know her but appreciated her for being there for me when I was crying. I grabbed her hand as I closed my eyes, and she laid her other hand on top of mine as we prayed.

"Hallelujah in this place tonight. Heavenly Father, we come before you no longer in our addictions and compulsive behaviors, but as the capable children You've made us to be. We now know, Lord, that we are more than conquerors. What the devil tried to use for bad, You have used it for good. Lord, we come in this place tonight asking that you remove all the chains from us that hold us captive and prevent us from living the life You've called for us. As we disperse for our breakout groups, we ask,

Lord, that You be with us in our hearts and minds and allow Your Word to penetrate our soles and help us change. In the mighty name of Jesus, we pray. Amen."

"Amen," the church repeated.

Everyone applauded. A few people shouted, "Hallelujah!" Tears turned into smiles. I was intrigued and confused at the same time. I had been going to church every Sunday since I was four years old, yet I never felt God like I felt Him in that place.

"Taneshia!" I heard someone yell. It was Joanne.

"Oh, my Goodness! Girl, this is the church you go to?" I asked, giving her a hug.

"Yes, girl. I saw you when you came in twenty minutes late," she said with an accusatory glare.

"My church aunt, Geneva, is here, too," I said, ignoring her comment and frantically looking around the room to find Geneva. I looked at my phone and saw a text from Geneva: *Taneshia, I had to leave early. Call me tomorrow.*

A part of me felt like I was off the hook. No need to stay for the rest if she wasn't there. I gave Joanne a kiss. "Okay, girl, I'm out! I only came because we're trying to start a group at my church like this one. I gotta go. You know I have a forty-mile drive ahead of me."

Joanne stared at me with pursed lips. "What you gonna do when you get home, have another threesome with Ben & Jerry? If you can even make it home. There's a McDonald's down the street. I'm sure you'll drive through before you get on the road."

Her words froze me into shock as people bumped my shoulder to get past me. *What did she say? This is what I'm talking about. I know this bitch did not just call me out. I like to eat, so what! It's better than having random sex with people I don't know like she does. Don't listen to her, Taneshia. Leave this building and handle your business.*

I wanted to follow my thoughts, but I was indignant. I couldn't believe she'd said that to me. "What is that supposed to mean?" I said with an attitude.

"Taneshia, listen, I know it sounds harsh, and I can only imagine the crazy thoughts you're having about me right now, but this is the problem. Did you not hear the speaker? Girl, you *are* the speaker! This is your time to get the help you need. You're already here. My self-awareness came from being here two times a week. You owe it to yourself, Taneshia. How long are you going to eat your problems away and then cry secretly in your room? You heard what the pastor said tonight. God doesn't want us to live that way, girl. I love you. The decision is yours."

As Joanne hugged me, I saw tears in her eyes. She gave me a kiss on the cheek and my hand and walked toward a door with a sign that read: LIVING WITH CODEPENDENCY. I stood there for a couple of minutes, crying and allowing myself to feel all the emotions that were running inside me. I felt angry, sad, embarrassed, and betrayed. I had told Joanne those things about me in confidence so she would listen, not throw it in my face at her discretion. I wasn't going to let her make me feel bad about coping with my life the best way I knew how. I started walking toward the exit. As I pulled my keys out of my purse, I found a candy bar. I pulled it out. I needed it. After being there listening to all those stories, I needed a way to release.

I walked to my car while dialoguing with my thoughts.

Joanne said there was a McDonald's close by. I'll google it when I get in the car. This is all too much. I'm happy these people have a place to come to and heal, but I'm fine. I don't need it. I go to church on Sunday, bible class on Wednesday, and I pray almost every night. That's enough. I know who God is. He loves me. So what if I can't say no without feeling guilty, and, yes, I do eat a lot, but I love to eat, and that's okay. God loves me just as I am.

It was much darker outside than it had been when I'd come in, and I struggled to find my car. "Shit! Where is it?" I yelled. I stopped walking and glanced over all the cars. "There it is. Thank you, God," I said.

"Hey, hey, hey!" I heard from the distance.

I turned around and saw the woman I sat next to in the church. "Damn, what does she want?" I whispered. "Hey, are you leaving, too?" I asked with a smile, hoping she couldn't sense my irritation.

"No, I went to my car to grab my twelve-step book. Are you leaving already?" she asked, looking at my keys and purse in my hand.

"Yes. I live about forty miles from here, and I have to get up early tomorrow."

"We all have to get up early tomorrow. You're here now. Might as well stay," she said with a laugh. "How long have you identified with being codependent?"

"I don't," I quipped, folding my hands. I didn't want to be mean to her, but I felt she was overstepping her boundaries. I ran support groups for years at my job. I knew what it was about. She was trying to engage me into going back inside, and it wasn't going to happen.

"Well, let me give you my phone number. If you ever want to talk more about it, call me. I know it's a lot to take in. When I first found out I was codependent, I was in denial, but after my husband spent all our savings on gambling and we lost our house, I had to admit I was a codependent and had enabled him in our relationship."

What the hell does "enable" mean? I thought. "Okay. Thank you."

I got into my car and pulled out of the parking lot. As I drove down the street, I remembered the candy bar I'd found in my purse. I grabbed it and desperately bit into it.

I am so glad you're out of that place. What the hell were you thinking, Taneshia? A support group? Girl, please. You're a social worker. You refer people to groups; you don't go yourself!

As I listened to my thoughts, I glanced to the right and saw McDonald's. "There it is!" I drove up to the drive-thru and looked at the menu. Not only was I hungry, but that meeting had my emotions on overload. Food was one of the few things that brought me comfort.

"Hello, may I take your order?"

"Yes, I would like a filet o' fish with a large fry and two chocolate chip cookies," I said, smiling at the intercom.

"Okay, will that complete your order?"

"No. Also, I would like a medium chocolate milk shake."

"Okay, that will be twelve dollars and sixty-nine cents at the first window."

I headed toward the window. *Damn, bitch! You just ate a Kit-Kat! Did you really need two cookies and a milkshake? You gonna be in a diabetic coma tonight.*

"Oh, well. I deserve it after tonight," I responded aloud.

When I got to the window and saw the food the cashier held out for me, I thought about what Joanne said. She was right. I did overeat, and even though I made excuses for myself, the reality was that I was diabetic. Joanne was worried about me because she knew overeating wasn't good for my diabetes and could make me sick. I gave the cashier my debit card and grabbed the bag. I set it on the passenger side and looked at it.

Don't try and feel bad now; you're the one who ordered all that crap. Your blood sugar numbers this morning were already through the roof. If you eat that, you might as well say goodbye to the thought of having your toes in the next ten years.

I started on the road and made a right onto the freeway. I drove in silence. My thoughts were talking to me so often, it felt like another person was sitting in the car. I looked at the McDonald's bag again with disgust. "Damn, Damn! I have to do something. This is crazy. Joanne is right, but I'm not going to a support group. Forget that! I facilitate support groups at work once a week!"

I occasionally glanced at the bag. *Taneshia, don't try and act like you're not hungry. You spent thirteen dollars on this food, and you're not gonna eat it? You know McDonald's tastes nasty once it gets cold.*

"I'm only going to eat the fish sandwich," I said.

I continued driving home, eating the sandwich and thinking. Before I knew it, I was in my driveway pulling up to the carport in front of my apartment. I looked at the bag and shook my head. "I'm throwing you in the garbage where you belong," I said, holding the bag and walking to the garbage can. I watched the food fall into the garbage, and a part of me wished I could grab it. I knew the taste of those chocolate chip cookies would make me feel better and forget about the craziness that happened that day.

Are you seriously thinking about getting those cookies out of the garbage? OMG! Taneshia, seriously?

I put my hand on my head. Suddenly, my face grew warm and tears came. "Lord, I need your help. I don't know what to do."

The next day, I threw on some sweatpants, a t-shirt, and tennis shoes and went to work. I was physically there but not mentally. I couldn't stop thinking about everything Joanne shared with me and what I had experienced that night. I realized food had become the way I coped with my life and ignored things I felt I couldn't change about myself. Maybe I did give others too much, and I wondered what my life would be like if I stopped saying yes when I wanted to say no, but I was afraid. What if people wouldn't like me anymore? How could I have friends if I said no to them when they needed me? Furthermore, how could I prove myself in a relationship with a man? And what about my parents and family? I couldn't dare say no or "I don't feel like it" to my mother. However, doing for everyone else all the time was showing up in my spirit, demeanor, and mood. I was exhausted, cranky, sad, and tired of not being free to live my own life.

I was also unhappy with my weight gain over the years. I had always been a thick girl but not fat. I was curvy-thick, not too big but not small. I was 5'9" and about 215 pounds, but because I was so tall, most people never suspected I weighed over 200 pounds. I knew it was time for me to make a change in my life, and I knew a therapist could help me.

Looking for a therapist was new to me and not an easy process. I didn't know anything about it. My job offered therapeutic services through an employment assistance program, so I followed the recommendation.

After writing down my contact information, the representative said, "Tell me the reason for your inquiry."

I didn't know what to say. *Do I tell her I broke down at a church event in front of people I didn't know, and I need help? Do I say I'm a struggling codependent? Perhaps I should just say I want someone to talk to.*

I decided to tell her I hadn't been feeling like myself and wanted someone to talk to.

As she screened me, I couldn't believe what I had done. Was I really being screened to see a therapist?

I continued an internal dialogue with myself for several seconds until I was interrupted by the representative asking if I was still there. I could feel the tears saturating my face. I couldn't speak, but I knew I had to say something. I softly said, "Yes."

The representative could tell I was crying. In a compassionate tone, she asked me what she could do for me. I first prepared to lie and say, "I'm okay. Please delete my information," but I couldn't. I felt something inside me say, *Stand up for you! Don't come all this way just to crash now. Tell her!*

I felt like I had stepped outside of myself and something or someone had taken over my vocal cords. "Please, help me. I'm seeking a therapist, preferably African American. I find myself crying daily, struggling to get out of bed, and I need someone to talk to." I felt relieved. I finally made a step for myself.

As I listened to the representative, I heard her words, but my internal dialogue started again. *Taneshia, what have you done? Has it really come to this? You feel like you need to speak to a therapist? All you need is God. Has He ever let you down before? You have to stop this.*

Aloud, I yelled, "Stop!" I was tired of having so many negative thoughts that controlled me and made me feel worthless.

The next day, I woke up feeling at ease, confident I made the right decision. It made me feel good knowing I finally put myself first. I didn't know what to expect. I had never met with a therapist before and, sadly, had no family or friends to ask about it. I was venturing out into new waters. Telling a stranger my business was taboo in my culture, but many times, the help I needed came from strangers. All my family lived in the South. My mother and I were isolated in California, so I had built a community of people who loved me like family, and I was hoping to add my therapist to my support circle.

I had scheduled my appointment for one p.m., and I made sure I was on time. I had the directions printed and payment ready. As I drove, I saw homeless people on the streets with mental health issues. Many of them were talking to themselves or wandering off.

My negative thoughts came back into my head. *Taneshia, therapy is for people like that. Are you really going through with this? This is insane! You are* fine! *Why go to a therapist?*

As I shook my head, I said, "Shut up! This is the best. I'm going!"

After driving around the office for fifteen minutes, I finally found a parking space. I ran into the building sad and confused. I couldn't find the door to her office because the labels weren't clear. I didn't know what to expect and, now, to make matters worse, I was late.

I finally found her door, knocked, and waited. "Hi, Dr. Jones?" I said with a smile.

"Yes, are you Taneshia?" she asked.

"Yes, yes I am," I said, happy I had chosen the right door.

She smiled firmly and told me to have a seat.

Dr. Jones was a slim African American woman. She had a mocha complexion and wavy hair. I was pleased to be working with a black female therapist. I knew I needed help, and I felt she may be able to identify with some of the issues I was experiencing because we shared the same cultural background.

"Sorry I'm late. I had so much trouble finding a parking space." I was still out of breath from running, and I was stuttering.

"That's unfortunate, but sessions will start promptly at the time we scheduled. I understand how difficult it can be to park in this area. There is a parking lot a few blocks down for future reference. For now, we will work with the time we have left for this session."

I began to think she might not be a good fit for me. I ran fifteen minutes late to everything—work, church, fun activities. How was I going to make it on time every week to see her? Maybe my thoughts were right. Maybe being late and unable to find parking were signs I shouldn't have been there. Nevertheless, I was there and ready to see what therapy had in store for me.

I looked around and got a feel for her office. It was set up nicely but different from what I'd imagined. There were two reclining chairs and a desk with a lamp and tissue on it. In the movies, I always saw a couch and pillow and someone lying back, looking up to the ceiling while telling their life story. This setup was interesting.

"Taneshia, my name is Dr. Cynthia Jones. I am happy you came today. Our first session will be an intake and a description of why you're here. You can share as much as you want or as little as you want; however, all the information we discuss will be helpful for me to get to know you. We can start off with you telling me a little bit about your upbringing and family history," she said.

I watched her put on her glasses and grab a pen. I wondered what to say. I didn't know what my response should be. I had gone through so many things in life and lost so much. I didn't know where to start.

My mother and I were nearly homeless several times, and my great-aunt, who had helped raise me, died when I was sixteen. My grandmother, who I had loved like my mother, died when I was nineteen. My life was one tragedy after another. I didn't know what part she wanted to hear.

I found myself stuttering. "Uh, okay. Well ... I was raised by my mother and great-aunt. My dad lives in another state, but we're close."

"Okay," she said, glancing at my body language. She eyed my shaking hands and likely noticed the quiver in my words. "Don't feel like you have to tell me everything today, Taneshia," she said compassionately. "We will discuss your family dynamic in future sessions. Just share with me why you came today and what you feel you need, if you know." She smiled.

My body felt numb, and I froze. I tried to speak, but I couldn't. *Future sessions? Damn, how many sessions does she think I'm going to need?* I thought.

She continued to write and look at me. I assumed she was used to people going numb in session. "Um, well, I think something is wrong. I don't know what's wrong, but it's something. I recently broke up with my boyfriend a few months ago. It was abrupt; he didn't even tell me why we broke up, and I think I eat for comfort," I said, embarrassed to admit it aloud to another person.

"Okay. Say more. Tell me the last time you felt this way."

"Last night, I went to a support group with my church aunt. We originally went there because we wanted to start a support group at our church, but once we got there, I saw a friend that mentioned to me that I always eat every time I'm sad." I paused because I noticed she was writing more.

She's writing on her notepad that you're crazy. You need to stop talking. Wrap up the thought, Taneshia, and get out of here! Don't forget you found this program through your job. What if she reports back to them?

I stared out the window and started to cry. I was called back by the sound of Dr. Jones calling my name. "Taneshia, Taneshia, tell me what you're feeling."

I looked at her, confused. *What does she mean 'feeling'? I feel sad, I guess. Doesn't she see the tears coming down my face?*

"What do you mean 'feeling'?" I asked.

"There is some tissue on the right side of you," she said, pointing to the box.

I grabbed one and continued crying while looking down at my lap. "I'm so tired of crying all the time. I cry sometimes all day."

"What is typically going on for you when you're crying? Paint a typical day for Taneshia. What does it look like?"

I looked at her in amazement. No one had ever given me the space to talk about myself before. It felt strangely comforting. I was used to helping everyone else. Someone showing interest in how I felt and what I was experiencing was foreign to me.

"I-I-I mean I don't know," I said. "Most days, I get up, drop my mom off at work, and I go to my internship for four hours, then I go to work for eight hours. I used to really like my job and the clients I serve. Now, I just go there for a paycheck. I am really good at helping people. I help all my family and my friends. I talk to family and friends a lot in the car while I'm driving."

She interrupted me. "Taneshia, tell me about you. What are you experiencing during the day emotionally? How do you feel?"

Wow, she's really serious.

"Taneshia, do you often know how you feel?" she asked patiently. I could tell she was trying to help me find the words to describe my feelings.

"No, no I don't. I usually help everyone else. I'm really good at helping others and taking care of people. My friend says that's a bad thing. That's another reason I'm here today," I explained, still crying and grabbing another tissue.

"What friend are you referring to?" Dr. Jones crossed her legs and seemed to be in tune with me.

"My, my friend Joanne. She broke up with her boyfriend and started going to support groups. Now, she thinks she's codependent and feels I am, too."

"Mmm, okay, I see. Share with me how you felt there. Taneshia, remember to take your time."

"Well, it felt like a regular church service, but they talked about their problems as if they were terrible and they were ashamed. We all have things about ourselves we don't like. No one will ever be perfect. I could see how meetings like that are helpful to drug addicts or alcoholics but not people like me and

Joanne. We're fine; we just have to practice saying no more. I admit my self-esteem isn't where it should be."

"How do you know that?" she asked looking at me closely.

"Well, the boyfriend I was referring to in the beginning, his name is Shawn. He recently left me alone in a hotel room in Las Vegas when I was supposed to be visiting him. I reached out to him for about two months before I found out he was engaged to someone else." My face felt warm and tears began to fall again.

"I see, Taneshia. I want to hear more about Shawn and this codependency group you attended; however, we only have ten more minutes left in our session. I would like to schedule another appointment with you. How do you feel about that?" she asked, pulling out a calendar and looking at me over her glasses.

It felt good for someone to ask me how I felt about decisions that included me. "Sure. I'm free most evenings next week," I said with a smile.

"Great, how is next Wednesday at five thirty p.m.?"

"I'll take it."

She stood and I did, too.

"Thank you, Taneshia, for coming in today, and I look forward to seeing you next week. If something comes up and you need to reschedule, please call or email me twenty-four hours prior to your appointment." She shook my hand, gave me her card, and closed the door after me.

I liked her, and I admired her ability to set boundaries. I liked the idea of seeing her regularly but started to worry about payment. My job would cover six sessions through the employment assistance plan, but then what would I do? I tried not to panic, but it was too late. My negative thoughts had already kicked in, and the internal dialogue was going full speed in my mind.

Taneshia, this is crazy. What are you going to do after six sessions? You barely have enough money to take care of your financial obligations, much less go to a therapist. You will have to end this after six sessions. Enjoy it while it lasts.

I ignored the thoughts because I was determined to continue. I had some money on my credit cards, and I could use them if I needed to. It was worth it.

That night, I lay in bed amazed at myself. I felt proud for seeing a therapist. It was nice to speak to someone about my problems. What a great experience to be able to talk to someone about my troubles then leave. I hoped I made a good decision.

CHAPTER 2

LONELY IN LAS VEGAS

The week flew by, and it was time to see Dr. Jones again. As I drove to her office after work, my thoughts started flooding my mind.

Are you truly going back there, Taneshia, for real? Girl, how are you going to be a therapist when you're seeing one? And did you forget that you have two papers due for school?

"I got this! I need to continue to meet with her," I said.

As I got closer to her office, I looked for the parking lot she had mentioned the previous week. I was determined not to be late. I found a parking space in front. "Yes!" I yelled, happy to be on time.

I walked up to her office and knocked on the door.

"Good afternoon, Taneshia. Come in," Dr. Jones said with a smile.

I sat and pressed the recline button on the right side of the seat. We smiled at each other.

"How have you been?" she asked while reclining her seat and picking up her pen and pad.

"I've been okay."

"Glad to hear that. First sessions can be hard. I'm glad you returned. Is this your first time in therapy?" she asked.

"No, I had a high school counselor, but it didn't feel like this."

"Mm hm. Say more about that. The *feelings* part of it," she said.

There goes that word again. What does she mean? I wondered. "Dr. Jones, what do you mean when you say 'feelings'? I don't feel anything about it," I said.

"You don't feel *anything*?" she said, surprised. "I see. Well, let's talk about what you want to discuss. Last week, you mentioned that you decided to consider therapy because your friend shared with you that she thinks you overeat. You also mentioned that you had a bad relationship with a man that ended abruptly. Would you like to discuss either of those topics today?"

"Okay."

"Great. Where should we start?"

I smiled in awe of someone caring so much about what was going on with me. It felt weird yet also very good. "Let's talk about Shawn. He's the real reason I feel I'm in this condition." I grabbed a tissue from the desk next to me.

"Taneshia," she said softly, "you're crying. Can you tell me why?"

"I-I-I don't know. I'm just tired."

"What does *tired* mean to you," she asked.

What? What does she mean? This is crazy. Words have their own meanings. Girl, you have a paper due at midnight. End this!

"Ugh!" I yelled. I was so tired of the negative thoughts constantly going through my mind. I felt my heart beating quickly. It seemed like my body and mind acted crazy every time I tried to get myself some help. First, at the support group, now at therapy. I exhaled and closed my eyes. My hands shook as tears flooded my face. I lay back in the chair and thought back to the day Shawn left me. Many thoughts crowded my mind. Would I be single forever? Would I ever get married or know what it's like to be loved unconditionally?

I didn't have the answers. Suddenly, Dr. Jones called me back to reality. "Taneshia, Taneshia," she said.

I turned toward her. I didn't know what to say. I decided to stop overthinking and just speak. "Nothing ever goes right in my life. I am thirty years old, and I still stay with my mother. I'm in graduate school to become a social worker and maybe a therapist, and now I *have* a therapist. I feel stupid! I feel like a fool! I feel tired of living this way. Always doing for other people and never myself. Everybody else always comes first."

"Okay! All right! Yes!" Dr. Jones smiled as if she'd just won the lottery. "Now, we are getting somewhere. Stay right there, right there in that feeling and say more. Tell me about Shawn and how you met," she said, writing in her pad.

"Uh, well, okay." I was confused because it appeared I had done something right, but I wasn't sure what. I paused in thought. To tell her what happened, I would have to relive the pain. I remembered each moment ...

It was my first time in Las Vegas. I was twenty-five with no cares in the world. The beautiful lights on the strip intrigued me, and I fell in love with them. I lost myself in the sweet aroma of all the hotels and casinos. It was like I had gotten away from all the pain and was finally experiencing peace.

My best friend and I were walking down Las Vegas Blvd when Shawn and I met. He was 6'3" with caramel skin, a slim build, and a Philly accent that melted my heart. He fit perfectly into my fantasy, and I fell in love. He was smart and such a gentleman. We spent hours talking until we watched the sun come up like we had known each other forever. I didn't want the moment to end, and Shawn appeared to feel the same. Before he left that morning, he asked me for my phone number. I was so happy. I felt like things were finally shifting in my life and I had met the man I would one day call my husband.

Shawn and I talked almost every week. Occasionally, he couldn't call, but I understood. He owned a music studio and was busy with his own album and his customers'. I knew I was a priority, even though he didn't show it all the time. We continued our long distance affair for four years, and I flew out to Vegas to see him about eight times during those years. But after a while, I noticed that Shawn sometimes went a month without calling me. I couldn't understand it, but I didn't think much of it. Every time we talked, things were great. We laughed and joked and sometimes even cried together about stressful things going on in our lives. I hoped that one day Shawn would mention moving to the Bay Area or me moving to Las Vegas to be with him, but I didn't want to burden him. I had faith that when the time was right and he was ready, the conversation would come up on its own.

During one conversation, I mentioned that we hadn't seen

each other in about a year. "Baby, I was wondering ... Maybe I can come see you soon," I said in a gentle tone.

"See me? Uh ... yeah, yeah, you can come, sweetie."

I heard the hesitation in his voice. "Is everything okay?" I asked, confused and somewhat upset.

"Yeah. It's all good. I'm just having a little money trouble right now."

"Well, I can pay for my own ticket and hotel. Would that make it easier?" I asked. I really wanted to see him, and I needed a break from my life.

"Yeah, sure, come in the next two weeks," he said.

"Okay, great. I love you."

"I love you, too, sweetie. Peace."

Two weeks passed, and it was time for me to visit Shawn. I woke up early to make sure I packed everything and wouldn't miss my flight. As I boarded the plane, my negative thoughts tried to discourage me.

What are you doing? This is crazy! Are you really going to Vegas again to see this guy? Turn around while you still can, fool! He hasn't even bothered to call you back in the last three days. What an idiot you are!

I softly whispered to myself, "I'm going, and things will be fine."

I texted my friends, hoping someone could send some healing words to encourage me. My friend Nikki sent me a response that led to her calling me.

"Hey, girl!" I said happily, hoping to mask the anxiety and fear in my voice.

"Hey. You on your way? Have you heard from him?"

Of course, she asked me that question out of all the questions she could have asked. "No, I haven't, but he told me to come."

"Okay. Be safe and call me when you get there."

I loved Nikki and knew she loved me. I could hear the fear in her voice. I was secretly worried, and so was she. I didn't know what to expect, but I knew I was going.

The thoughts started again, louder this time.

Taneshia, there is still time to get off the plane. This is crazy.

As I looked for a seat, I knew I had to ground myself. I whispered positive affirmations. I looked around frantically, hoping no one saw me talking to myself. I closed my eyes, said a prayer, and dropped my bag under my seat. I put my headphones on and found a track on my phone's playlist called "Mr. Yeah" by The Dream. Every time I heard it, I was reminded of the great time I had when I first met Shawn and every time after. As the plane elevated, I could feel my thoughts leave my mind. I found my happy place.

I landed in Las Vegas at 2:30 p.m., and it felt good to be back, away from my life, problems, and everything that reminded me of pain. The sounds of the slot machines were calming bells to my ears. I turned my phone on, and multiple text messages poured in from the friends I texted before boarding. I had a voicemail from Shawn! I smiled eagerly and felt elated. As I listened to his deep voice through the phone, I imagined his lips on mine. The first time I kissed him, it felt so right and perfect, and the first time we made love, he sent my body to the clouds. I felt that way every time we talked. Although our love was long distance, it would only be temporary, until we both found our way. We were young. I was twenty-nine, and he was thirty-four. We had full lives ahead of us. But there was nothing wrong with spending time together in the meantime. In his voicemail, he mentioned he had to work and would meet me at the hotel. It didn't matter to me. I was happy just knowing he was coming and I would see him.

I headed to baggage claim feeling free and in love. I couldn't wait to wrap my arms around him, stand on my toes, and give him a big kiss. He told me he would be busy and wouldn't be able to pick me up from the airport. Over the years, my credit cards had become my best friends, so I easily reserved a car. I drove down Las Vegas Blvd admiring the beauty of the street. It felt good to be away. I'm sure people wondered why my smile was so big. I didn't care. They didn't know my life or the joy being away brought me.

I had reserved a room at the Hilton for Shawn and me. The room was amazing, and I was eager to get into the Jacuzzi. I set my bags down and slowly placed the rose petals I brought on the bed in the shape of a heart. I took my clothes off and embraced my body. I knew my hands weren't going to be the only pair on me, and I eagerly awaited the feel of his body next to mine.

I ran a bath in the Jacuzzi, added soap, and stepped in, washing every part of my body. I often closed my eyes and imagined how nice Shawn's hands would feel on each part of me.

I heard my phone ringing. With a grudge, I got out of the tub to answer it. It was Shawn. "I'm running behind, sweetie. I'll see you later tonight. Are you okay?"

Later tonight? I didn't understand. He knew I was coming. *He hadn't made plans to spend time with me?* "Okay. What time do you think you'll be here?" I asked with a frown.

"I'm not sure. I'll call you when I get done working."

I was mad as hell, but when I opened my mouth, I only said, "Okay, baby." I hung up, confused.

As I gazed out the window, my negative thoughts flooded my conscious.

All this money you paid to come out here and be with him, and he's running late? I told you to turn around. You never listen to me. This is going to be a disaster.

I walked back to the tub and got in. This time, I soaked a bit, telling myself not to worry. He was coming, and everything would be fine. I spent another fifteen minutes in the tub before getting out. I had purchased a new outfit and gotten my hair done. I slid on the cute beige top and booty shorts that made my figure look amazing. I put my heels, bracelet, and earrings on and fixed my hair.

By 6:30 p.m., I still hadn't heard from Shawn since we'd talked at five. I called him back, and the phone went to voice-mail. I left a message telling him I was waiting for him and to let me know when he was on the way. I texted him the address to the hotel and the room number.

I sat on the bed watching television and staring at my phone. Where was he? It was 7:45. I was getting worried and upset. I called Shawn again. This time, the phone went straight to voicemail. I left another message. He called me back around eight, telling me he was in traffic and would be there in an hour. I said okay and continued to wait.

I was starving, so I ran to the store to grab some snacks and came back to the hotel. It was 9:30. Where was he? I called back, and he answered the phone angry this time. "Taneshia, what's up! I told you I'm busy."

"Where are you? I've been waiting for you for hours, Shawn!"

I was almost in tears, upset because I was talking to him on the phone and not holding him in my arms.

"I don't think I can make it. I have things to do, and I can't get away," he said nonchalantly.

"What? Shawn, I barely had money to come see you this time, and you didn't bother to help me, either! We haven't seen each other in a year, and now you're telling me I came all the way out here to see you, and you're not coming?" Tears filled my eyes. I wished I would've listened to the thoughts that told me to turn around when I was on the plane.

"Taneshia, I have to go."

And that was it. He hung up, and I was left alone in a hotel room in Las Vegas.

I sat on the bed staring at the ceiling, crying, feeling angry and alone. I had sacrificed my time and body for someone who couldn't even show up for me. I lay on the bed, grabbed the pillows and sobbed. The sight of the flower petals on the bed made me cry more. I couldn't believe this was happening to me. All my dreams of being with him, being kissed and touched, were gone. I was alone, although it didn't stay that way for long. My negative thoughts soon joined me.

Isn't this a mess? Are you happy now? Here we are, alone like always, except, this time, we're out four hundred dollars and in Las Vegas! When are you going to learn that no one loves you, Taneshia? Did you really think you had a boyfriend in Vegas? Don't make me laugh. Don't just lay here and cry. Get yourself the hell out of here!

This time, I listened to the thoughts. They were all I had. I found myself having a full internal dialogue.

Oh Lord, am I going crazy? Have these thoughts turned into voices? I took a deep breath. *You're just going through something,* I told myself. *Don't overreact.*

Suddenly, my self-assurance was disrupted.

You are *crazy. Now you're here in Las Vegas alone. Did you really think he was coming? You haven't been able to get ahold of him, girl! He called you and left a twenty-second message, and, suddenly, that was supposed to make up for it? Someone who cares about you does that? Wake up, Taneshia! He has no respect for you. How can someone so smart be so gullible? Call Southwest Airlines, fool! Get the hell out of here!*

I followed the voice's instruction and quickly searched for my credit card and flight information on my phone. I dialed Southwest Airlines' customer service. "Good evening. Thank you for calling Southwest Airlines. How can I help you?"

"Hi, my name is Taneshia Johnson. I'm calling to see if I can get an earlier flight from Las Vegas to Oakland, California."

"May I have your confirmation number?"

"Yes, it's 6KJQ19."

As she paused to look up my number, I desperately hoped she found another flight that left that night. I couldn't stay there. Between my emotions and negative thoughts, I felt like I was going crazy.

My thoughts were ringing in my ears louder than usual. *What if she can't find a flight? What are you going to do?*

"Shut up!" I said. I was paranoid, worried that not only the people in the next room would think I was crazy, but also the representative on the phone. As I attempted to end the conversation with myself, I could hear someone talking. I realized the voice was the representative.

"Hello, ma'am?" she said, sounding confused.

"Yes, yes. I'm here." I hoped she didn't hear me talking to myself.

"I regret to say I can't find a flight equivalent to the price you paid."

"Okay," I said sadly. "Thank you."

I hung up with tears streaming down my face.

So, what now? Here we are lonely and alone. Round of applause, Taneshia. You messed up again! Big time!

I cried as loud as I could. I didn't know what to do. What *could* I do? Shawn wasn't coming. That was reality.

I needed some support. I wanted someone to help me feel better and distract me from the pain and my thoughts. I remembered that one of my best friends was in Vegas for a business conference. As the phone rang, I prayed he answered.

"Hey, boo!" he said happily.

I stuttered, trying to talk over my tears. "He isn't coming, Jordan," I managed.

"Okay, boo. Where are you?" he said in a soft, calming tone. I could tell he knew I was hurting.

"I'm at the Hilton in Henderson, Nevada."

"Do you have a car? How far is that from the strip?"

"It's about ten miles. I can drive to you."

"Okay, boo. I'm at the Paris Hotel. Meet me here," he said.

I immediately ran to the restroom. I wiped my tears with a washcloth, put some lip gloss on, grabbed my bag, and left.

As I drove down the strip, Drake's song, "Wrong Thing to Do" started playing. He told a story about liking a girl but not having genuine feelings for her. He knew it was wrong to lead her on and decided to end the relationship without much discussion. I started crying again. Was that how Shawn felt, like he couldn't be open and tell me he didn't feel the same about me and wanted to stop seeing me? I thought he and I had started off as friends. We'd spent hours on the phone for years telling each other our deepest pains and disappointments. We had shared four years together. How could he just leave like that and not even tell me why? I was so confused.

I pulled up to the Paris Hotel, and the bright lights caught my attention. I remembered how much I loved Vegas. I didn't want those feelings to end just because of Shawn. I parked my car and headed to the casino to meet Jordan. He and I had been friends since I was sixteen years old. He had big dreams of owning his own business, and this was his first business trip. I was proud of him for his accomplishments, but I felt bad about raining on his parade.

I cried on his shoulder, still in a state of shock. He gave me five dollars for the slot machine and asked me what happened. We played the machines and drank as I gave him the play-by-play.

Jordan was livid but empathetic. "I can't believe this nigga left you here like this, boo. I love you, and I'm glad you remembered I was here and wasn't ashamed to call me."

"Thanks," I said while holding his hand.

Should I tell him about the thoughts I had in the hotel? I asked myself. I quickly decided it was inappropriate and chose not to share.

We laughed and joked. It felt good to be with my friend. We walked the strip for a few hours until we grew tired and decided to head back to our hotels.

I drove on the freeway, nervous about driving so late in a

foreign city. Those feelings of abandonment and loneliness returned. Suddenly, my thoughts came back into my head.

This is so sad. I can't believe he did this! We're stuck and left alone in Vegas. You're going to call him again, right? Check his Facebook account. What is he doing? He's likely with another woman. You are aware of that, aren't you? Please don't tell me you believe this working late crap. As soon as you get to the room, you need to look him up on Facebook. As a matter of fact, do it before you get there. He owes you an explanation.

The thought was right. Shawn did owe me an explanation. I pulled up in front of the hotel, parked the car, and immediately jumped onto social media. But his account was gone! *What did he do with it?* I texted him. It was two a.m., but I didn't care. He didn't text back. I called him. No answer. I called again. Nothing.

I searched my purse for my room key and walked into the hotel. I entered the elevator with my head down and tears in my eyes. I couldn't believe I was living this madness. I felt as if my existence didn't matter to anyone. *Why was I put on this earth?* Every painful and negative memory came to me. I sat in that hotel room feeling abandoned and alone, but for some strange reason, it felt familiar.

As I cried, I felt a split happening within me. The thoughts that had turned into a voice now had a face. I could see her—an image of me. She and I cried together. Warm tears ran down my face as I lay there holding the pillow tight, imagining someone was holding me, but no one was there. Just my thoughts and me.

<hr/>

I opened my eyes and looked at Dr. Jones. I knew I had to

say something, but just remembering everything that happened brought so much pain. I couldn't find the words to explain what a fool I had been to think someone loved me after only meeting him eight times in a four-year period. I felt like an idiot. All I could do was look at her and cry.

"Taneshia, how did it make you feel when Shawn left you?" she asked.

"It was hard," I said, wiping my tears. "Real hard. How could someone do that to another human being? He abandoned me just like my dad and everybody else."

"Taneshia, let's pause. How does the incident with Shawn connect to your dad?" She scribbled something in her notebook.

I grew tired of watching her write notes. "What are you writing about me in that notebook?" I asked with a scowl.

"I'm writing incidents and memories you share with me so I can help you connect everything later. Is that okay with you?"

Wow, there she goes again asking me how I feel. It felt so good to be heard and validated. I couldn't be angry with her anymore. "Yeah, yeah, that's fine." I nodded.

"Taneshia, we are out of time; however, it is important to me to hear about the connection you've made between your dad and feeling abandoned by Shawn. Do you have fifteen more minutes to talk about this?"

"Hmm ... I don't know. How does payment for extra time work? Will I have to pay more?" I asked nervously.

"No, you don't have to pay extra for more time. You touched on something significant to your feelings and how they connect to how you feel about yourself." Dr. Jones took her glasses off and looked down at her notepad. "Taneshia, you mentioned that you're aspiring to be a therapist; is that still correct?"

"Yes, yes, it is." I wondered what she was hinting at.

"The moment you've experienced today is called a break-through, a moment in therapy when the client says something that can lead to them realizing more about themselves and what they need to heal, and, in your case, shares an emotion," she explained smiling.

"I did?"

"Yes, you did. You mentioned feeling abandoned."

"Feeling abandoned is an emotion?" I asked in shock.

"Yes, yes, it is." She nodded. "It's a complex emotion; never-theless, it is an emotion."

"Wow!" I said in awe.

"So tell me about feeling abandoned by your dad."

"My mother and father were not involved when I was born, and my father had another family. Most of my life, I felt like a burden to both parents but definitely my dad. It was obvious his family didn't approve of my birth. I don't have many memories of them coming to see me or calling me, and when I ask, they often say things like, 'There was a lot going on when you were born' or 'We didn't know what to do about you.'" I grabbed some tissues to catch my tears. "I can remember when I was eight years old, my grandpa died. That was the first time I had seen him in my life. It was like looking at an older version of my dad. I remember family members making me feel like I was in the way and shouldn't have been there."

"Taneshia, I am so sorry. I can imagine that was painful for you. How did those statements they made make you feel?"

"Like no one wanted me, and I was in the way. I'm a good person. I don't understand why my dad's family took so long to see that. I didn't ask to be here. It's not my fault! How long am I going to suffer for something that's not my fault? God put me here, not me. I really want to be a part of the family and do things with them, but I'm not going to keep fighting or proving myself. It just feels hopeless and exhausting. I know my dad loves me. I mean he calls me, and I visit him regularly. He shows up to graduations and stuff, but we don't have the deep connection I wish we had."

"I see. When you say connection, what are you referring to?"

"He tells me general stuff. We don't talk about much, and when I try to get advice, he often just encourages me to pray. I wish we spent more time and knew things about each other like our favorite color, foods he likes to eat, those kinds of things. It's weird, you know?"

"I see. So when Shawn left you in the hotel, you mentioned that you had to wait for him, and you thought he wasn't going to show up. You also stated that several times during your four-year interaction, he'd gone weeks without calling you. Did that seem strange to you?" she asked.

"No. We usually talked about once a week or once every two weeks."

"Mm. I see. How often do you talk to your dad?" she asked, this time, writing in her notebook.

"Now, I talk to my dad about two or three times a week, but when I was younger, I talked to him about once a month, occasionally twice a month. Sometimes I would think to call him, but I didn't want to bother him. He's always busy," I said.

"Bother?" she asked, surprised. "You mentioned earlier that you often felt you were 'in the way' while growing up. Did you feel that way with Shawn?"

I looked at her with confusion. What was she talking about? "No, I never felt in the way with Shawn." I sat up attentively in my seat, eager to see where she was going with this.

"Okay. Another statement you made was that you and Shawn had seen each other about eight times in a four-year period. How often do you see your dad?" she asked, writing again.

"I used to see my dad every year. I spent every summer with him, but it's harder now that I'm in graduate school."

"When is the last time you saw him?"

"I saw him about two years ago."

"Mmm. I see. Is this common for you and him?"

"Yes."

"Taneshia, I see a possible correlation here between Shawn and your father. May I share?"

I looked down at my hands and feet, which were shaking uncontrollably. "Okay," I said.

"Taneshia, I wonder if you feel abandoned by Shawn and possibly your dad because you have learned that relationships don't require much effort or communication. I don't want to offend you, but your relationship with your father is not normal. I'm happy to hear that you and he have found a way to make it work considering he lives in another state. However, it seems your father and you share an insecure/dismissive attachment. Do you know what that is?"

"No."

"It's an attachment style that develops when someone is kind of there for you, but their time is quick, inconsistent, and, most of the time, unfulfilling. They are there for a while, then they leave. How does that sound?"

"Wow, it sounds accurate! So you're saying my dad is emotionally unavailable to me?"

"Yes, that is exactly right, and, in turn, you may have learned growing up that your feelings don't matter and you're not important. So you don't question when a person—in this incident, Shawn—is inconsistent with phone calls. Because growing up, your conversations with your dad were not consistent. How does that sound?" she asked.

I started to cry. "Yes, wow! I am so messed up," I confessed.

"You're not messed up, Taneshia. You're learning about yourself, and that's called healing. We have to end for today. Let's continue to talk about Shawn next week."

"Thank you," I said, grabbing my purse and shaking her hand.

"You're welcome. Take care, and see you next Wednesday at five thirty p.m."

CHAPTER 3

JUST ME AND ME

Growing up, I often felt I wasn't worth much to my biological father, so why would another man make time for me? Maybe I was stupid to think any man would feel I was special enough to sacrifice himself or his time. Maybe Dr. Jones was on to something. Maybe I was picking men who were emotionally unavailable, and I didn't know the signs of real love. I felt confused, but I also felt that therapy was helping me, and I didn't want to stop going.

The following Wednesday arrived, and it was time to meet Dr. Jones. I left work exactly at five p.m. and found a parking space a block away from her office. "Yes," I said happily. This made two weeks in a row I found parking easily. I walked up to her office door and rang the doorbell.

"Hello, Taneshia. So good to see you," she said, smiling.

"Hi!" I felt chipper and ready to talk. I threw my bag down, hopped onto the seat, and pushed the recliner button to kick my feet up. I was hoping to have another breakthrough.

"I thought we might take this session to wrap up where we left off about Shawn," she said, placing her hands on her knees.

Oh snap! She wants to hear what happened after *Shawn. Girl, you know no one can ever know about that. You damn near went crazy. Hell, if you're honest with yourself, you* did *go crazy! What if she writes a letter to your job? Think before you talk!*

My thoughts were too loud in my head. I silenced them and decided to tell her the truth no matter what my thoughts said.

The next day, I prepared myself to fly back home. I had been up most of the night, lying in the same bed I thought I would be sharing with Shawn. As I dropped each rose petal in the trash, tears ran down my face. I was still in shock. I wasn't worth him making time for me? If that was true, and apparently it was, maybe that was how other men in my life felt, too.

During the plane ride home, I reflected on the devastation of that weekend. All I could do was cry for the entire one-hour-twenty-five-minute flight. I wondered if I could forget it happened. I was so deep in my thoughts that I didn't realize when the plane landed in Oakland.

I tried to gather my thoughts as we deplaned. I went to the restroom and wiped my face with a wet towel. The cold water felt good on my swollen eyes, which were rose colored from crying so much. As I looked at myself in the mirror, I had more thoughts.

You are so pitiful. Are you really going to allow him to do this to you? Call him! Think about all the money you're losing, and for what? All because you don't know how to stand up for yourself!

I surveyed the restroom to ensure no one else was in there with me. I looked in the mirror and yelled, "Shut up! I *am* going to call! Don't you think I know how much money I've lost?" I paused. *Oh, my goodness. Am I actually talking to myself?*

I heard footsteps coming into the restroom. I immediately packed my purse, grabbed my luggage, and walked out. I started my way to the train station. My phone was on and buzzing constantly. It seemed like hundreds of texts were coming in at once. What would I tell people?

Well, of course you're gonna have to lie! You can't tell people what really happened.

Was I going crazy? I was a social worker. Had I turned from a mental health professional into a person who struggled with her own mental health? If so, what did all of it mean? My thoughts were yelling in my ear and seemed to have taken the form of a real person who was standing in front of me, mad as hell that she was going through this experience.

Suddenly, I realized I had blacked out for longer than I realized and missed my stop. I exited the train and attempted to gather my thoughts at least enough to determine where I was and how I was going to get home. I saw signs that read San Leandro Station. Damn! I had gone too far. San Leandro was thirty miles away from home.

As I walked to the other side of the train station platform, I thought about Shawn. I wondered what he was doing and if he felt guilty for what he did to me. I sent him a text message: *Shawn, I made it back home. Please call me. I forgive you. Just tell me what happened.*

After I hit the send button, I realized I had sent him a text as if I were the one in the wrong. He faked on me! Ruined my vacation! Ruined my life! Most importantly, he killed my fantasy of being with him and not living my real life, which was full of pain, sorrow, and loneliness.

The next day was rough. I attempted to get up and get ready for work, but I couldn't find my way out of bed. Every time I got up, it felt like fifty-pound weights were attached to my ankles. I lay in bed crying and calling Shawn, hoping he'd pick up. He never did. I kept hoping I would get a text from him explaining that he had been in jail, the hospital, or some crazy scenario that had prevented him from calling me. Eventually, I had to face reality—He had *chosen* to leave me in a hotel alone and abandon me just like everyone else. Abandonment had become a comfortable space for my existence.

Days turned into weeks. Over time, my thoughts calmed down, and I began living with the truth that I was alone with no clue about how to get out of my feelings. I was just existing, putting clothes on that didn't fit or match. I didn't groom myself like I normally would. Everything was a mess in my life.

Only the grace, love, and mercy of God sustained me. I came in late to work, barely meeting with my clients and spending more time crying and listening to gospel music than working. An average day consisted of me sitting on the edge of my bed for thirty minutes, crying, driving to work in a daze, and putting a smile on my face to counsel clients when I didn't even know how to give myself what I needed. I felt so alone.

I often forgot about projects and papers for school. My graduate school friends helped me stay on track. Many times, they asked me what was wrong. I froze, unsure of what to say. How could I tell people that the person I thought loved and cared about me had left me in a hotel room? How could I explain that all my feelings of being in love had dwindled away? Luckily, it was the last year of my graduate program, so it was easy to agree with everyone else and call my feelings "senior blues" or exhaustion. I knew it was more than that and so did God, but I wasn't ready to share it with anyone yet.

As the days went on, I was still obsessed with Shawn. I couldn't understand why he left me. Was I a horrible person who wasn't deserving of love? What had I done to cause it? Several of my close friends tried to console me. While talking to one of them on the phone, I was triggered to look up Shawn's Facebook page. After suspecting that he'd blocked me from his FB page and, likely, his phone, I created a new FB account just to confirm. And he had, indeed, blocked me.

When I pulled up his page, it was immediately apparent that he was engaged to another woman. My whole heart dropped into my chest as I cried to my friend on the phone. I couldn't believe it. Not only was he ignoring me, but he had gone and made a new life for himself without me. Who was this woman who had taken my joy and love away from me? I examined her, the shape of her face, her eyes, her body. She disgusted me. Her figure reminded me of the cartoon character SpongeBob Squarepants. She represented everything I had lost. Shawn was my everything. He was my happiness.

I told my friend I had to go. I found myself staring at the computer screen, dissecting her, trying to figure out how she became more important to him than me. I was slowly going into a dark place. It reminded me of where I'd gone when I was in that hotel in Vegas.

My thoughts began communicating with me. I could hear them ringing loudly in my head. I got up from the bed and paced my room. My mother was in the other room, so I couldn't scream, cry out, and punch the walls like I wanted to. How could this be happening to me? Why had he left me for her? She wasn't even pretty.

I couldn't contain my rage. Before I knew it, I collapsed on my bed, crying and screaming into my pillow until I fell asleep. I woke up to find that it was seven a.m. I had forgotten to set my alarm clock, and I was late for work. I immediately called my supervisor and made up a lie about being stuck in traffic and needing more time. I didn't want to tell the truth, that I had been crying all night and fell asleep to the sound of my heart breaking.

As I ran around my room frantically looking for something to wear, the image of Shawn and his girlfriend invaded my mind. I stepped into the shower and felt the warm water soothing my puffy eyes. I ran the loofa sponge across my body and imagined Shawn's hands. I could remember his touch. His hands felt so good embracing my body. I stood in the shower for a while, rubbing the loofa across each part of me. Tears drained my eyes as I wondered if I would ever be touched by a man again.

Most mornings started that way. I made it to work most days. I'd smile during the day and cry myself to sleep at night. Soon, I could no longer keep up a happy façade, and my outer appearance matched my inside. My life had been taken over by a storm. My thoughts came back in full form, and they wouldn't turn off. I was being mentally beaten every day.

I woke up to thoughts telling me to lie back down. I was

nothing, worthless, and no one wanted me. I was only here to make everyone else's dreams come true, and I was to never have my own. I struggled to match my outfits and make sure I didn't have on mix-matched shoes. I hoped no one noticed.

One thing I always admired about myself was my ability to overcome and persevere. I was determined to find my way through my hardships. I was broken but functioning. I wasn't going to allow my situation to destroy my future.

My struggle at school mirrored my struggle at work. Often, I did my research papers the night before, hoping my past knowledge and work experience would be enough to make my papers decent. God was always with me. Every paper that might have deserved a C or D was graded with an A. I was shocked. Even in my weakest moment, I was still being carried by God despite how sad and disappointed I'd been with Him.

I couldn't understand why He let all these things happen to me. I didn't have the answer and felt as if God abandoned me when it came to love. I didn't know what to do. *Should I just accept that I will be alone?* The terms I had learned—"codependency" and "people pleasing"—came to my mind. I assumed that maybe caregiving for people was going to be my life. I couldn't say no to anyone. My parents, friends, coworkers, sometimes even my clients. It was like this nagging feeling that if I said no and didn't give people what they wanted from me, no one would love me, and I would be alone. In turn, even after giving everything I had to Shawn, I still ended up alone.

I lost myself in reminiscence as I stared out the window again.

"Taneshia, look at me. Let's focus on being present during sessions. What is happening for you when you look out the window? Tears come down your face, but you don't say anything. Do you often tell people how you feel?" Dr. Jones asked.

My tears trapped my vocal cords. I shook my head.

"I see. Well, let's practice that."

"I have a lot of thoughts all the time. Sometimes they taunt me all day. They say such mean things to me, and it makes me cry," I said.

"Mmm," she said, writing. "Thoughts ... I see. Were you having these thoughts when Shawn didn't show up?"

"Yes. They told me I was stupid for going, and then later, when I discovered he was engaged to be married, they told me I would never be with anyone. Maybe they're right." I blew my nose and wiped my eyes. I looked back at Dr. Jones to see her writing, this time quickly.

"Taneshia, unfortunately, we have run out of time. Oftentimes during session, you seem to go into a daze for long periods of time. Do you hear my voice when I call your name?"

"I do, but sometimes my thoughts are louder. It's almost like a voice in my head that's constantly telling me everything I do or say outside of helping other people is selfish and stupid. They tell me my life is about my accomplishments, but life should be fun, right? Not always struggling, trying to figure things out. I don't know how to quiet the voice. I gave up a long time ago."

"I see. Well, how about we partner to figure out how. Next week, same time?" she asked with a smile.

I smiled back as I wiped my tears. "Yeah, same time."

"Okay, take care," she said as she closed the door.

CHAPTER 4

CODEPENDENCY

As I walked to my car, I got a phone call. It was one of my clients. I had forgotten to turn my work cell off. "Ugh, it's six thirty p.m. What does she want?" I cleared my throat and forced a smile before picking up the phone. "Hi, this is Taneshia."

"Hey, girl! OMG, I am so glad you answered the phone. Taneshia, I know I have an appointment with you tomorrow, but I was wondering if we could meet tonight. I'm already by your office."

What? Is she serious?

Although I was only ten minutes away, I refused to go back.

But what if she really needs you? You know she's homeless. That's messed up. Wow, you know you were raised better than this. What are you going to rush home to, another hot date with Ben & Jerry? Just see her right now and come to work later.

This was one of the few times my thoughts had a good point;

it would be nice to sleep in a little the next morning. "Okay, meet me at the Starbucks on Eighth Street. I will be there in about fifteen minutes," I said with a grudge.

"Yay! Taneshia, you are a rock star. Thank you!"

Rock star ... Yeah, you're a rock star, all right. A rock star who's an idiot. Did you forget you had to pick your mom up from work? This isn't going to turn out well for you, girl.

"Damn! Oh, my God!" I had forgotten about my mom. I had to call her and let her know. I dialed her number, not knowing what her response would be. "Hey, Mom; it's me. I forgot I have a late appointment."

There was a long pause. Long pauses were never good. They usually meant she was upset. I felt my heart skip a few beats. My palms started to sweat, and my hands were shaking. *Lord, what is this?* I saw a bus bench next to me. I had to sit.

"Taneshia, that's fine. Call me when you're closer to the house. Bye."

"Thank God she wasn't upset," I said to myself. The bus stop was right in front of a cupcake shop I really liked. Starbucks was still about five blocks away. I wasn't going to make it. I called my client back. "Hey, can you meet me at the cupcake shop on Telegraph Street? I'm not going to make it to Eighth."

"You didn't get my text? My baby daddy is going to meet me. I can't make it. I'll call you tomorrow."

"What? But I already changed my plans for you," I spat. She hadn't even bothered to call me and tell me she wasn't coming, and here I was feeling like I was going to pass out trying to make time to see her.

"Sorry, but I still need help finding an apartment. I will call you tomorrow," she said and hung up.

I sat there for a while feeling my heart pounding in my chest. I didn't know what to do. Whatever these episodes were, they only came when I was stressed, and they didn't last long.

I walked inside the cupcake shop and looked around. Each cupcake was made to perfection and looked so good. They had all kinds: chocolate, vanilla, butterscotch, strawberry, double chocolate, and so much more. I felt like I was in heaven. I couldn't leave without picking one up. As the lady behind the register approached me, I tried to appear like I wasn't in pain. I stood straight, removed my hand from my chest, and put a smile on my face.

"Can I help you," she asked with her hands on her hips.

I didn't like her attitude, but I didn't care because I needed that cupcake. "Yes. May I have one chocolate, one double chocolate, and one strawberry crème cupcake, please?"

As she put each cupcake into a box, I slowly started feeling better. My heart was still pounding, but it wasn't as bad as it was earlier.

"Twelve fifty," she said.

I pulled out my debit card and swiped it. She handed me the box, and I walked out. I pulled the strawberry crème out first. As I started to eat the cupcake, I could smell the fresh strawberries. I took small bites at first, but when I tasted how good they were, I went ahead and put the whole cupcake in my mouth. People were looking at me walk down the street stuffing cupcakes into my mouth, but I didn't care. My heart wasn't flying out of my chest, and my palms weren't sweating. I was at peace.

I heard my phone ringing. I didn't want to answer it; I just wanted to stay in the moment of eating my cupcakes and enjoying the peace. But whoever it was kept calling. I stopped at a bench to put the cupcake box down and see who was calling. It was Joanne. We hadn't spoken since that night we argued at the codependency group. I didn't know what to say to her, but she was my friend, so I answered.

"Hey, girl. How are you?"

"Hey, Taneshia. I miss you, girl. How have you been? I hope you're not still upset about that night.

I tried to talk but I couldn't. Tears began flooding my eyes, and I felt knots in my throat. "Joanne, I think you're right. I do use food as a comfort, and, lately, I have these episodes where my heart starts beating fast. My life is just all over the place. I don't know what I'm going to do. Shawn left me. I have nothing ..."

"Taneshia, girl, you are going to make me cry. It's going to be all right. Why don't you come to the group with me tomorrow? What did you decide to do about therapy?" she asked. I could tell that she had also started crying.

"I have gone to her about three times now. Girl, she says I have an emotionally unavailable relationship with my dad. Is that crazy or what? My dad loves me!"

"Taneshia, she didn't say he didn't love you. You and your dad have worked hard to maintain a relationship considering the distance between you both. What she said was he was emotionally unavailable, and that, my friend, is true. Your dad loves you, but you have said yourself that as soon as you start crying and talking about the past, it's too much for him. There's nothing wrong with that. It doesn't mean he doesn't love you. He just can't handle all the emotional stuff from so far away. I'm sure it's hard on him, too, being so far away from you while you're in pain, but let me stop acting like the therapist. What else did she say?"

"She said that the relationship with Shawn was always weird."

There was a long pause.

I started to get worried. "Hello, hello, Joanne?"

"Yep, yep, I'm still here."

"Did you hear what I said?"

"Yep, I did."

"And ... So what do you think?"

"Taneshia, you're so sensitive these days. Let me first do a safety check. Where are you?"

"Safety check ... Girl, stop playing. I am not about to hurt myself based on what you say!"

"Okay, okay. You wanna put your big girl panties on, then, so we can have a real conversation?"

"Come on with it!" I said.

"Taneshia, Shawn was all in your imagination. That man never wanted you. The whole relationship was in your mind. He looked at you like a friend who gave up the booty. I don't know how many times I have to tell you this—You are codependent! Taneshia, you do whatever anybody wants you to do, not because you're naïve, but you fear they won't love you or like you if you don't. That is codependence. There is power in admitting it, Taneshia. It's step number eight in the twelve-step book. Did you read it yet?"

"Joanne, I'm losing reception. I have to go," I said and hung up.

I didn't want to hear all that crap! Here I was rushing home because my client hadn't shown, and to top it off, I dropped one of my cupcakes while trying to answer the phone to talk to Joanne. Dealing with the fact that I might be codependent on top of all the other problems I had was just too much. All I wanted to do was go home, eat, and go to bed. Although I was upset with Joanne, what she'd said brought me some clarity and relief. *If* I was codependent, that meant there may be a cure for it. Maybe I could go to the groups with her and get a better understanding of what it was.

I made it home and went over the twelve-step book like Joanne suggested. After reading a few pages, I concluded that people didn't love me for who I was; they loved me because of what I did for them. I had spent the first thirty years of my life overcompensating and caregiving for family, friends, co-workers, and clients. No wonder I was exhausted all the time. Listening to everyone's problems and being empathetic was all too much. I dreamed about focusing on myself and no one else. I was living a horrible life. But it was the only way I knew how to live—being a caregiver, people pleaser, and being in control.

Learning about codependency became fun to me. It was painful to read because it made me reflect on how many years I had spent focusing on other people and not myself, but it also made me feel slightly at peace. I found some great books by experts on codependency like Ross Rosenberg and Melody Beattie. Melody's book *Codependency No More* became one of my favorites and gave me a foundation for exactly what code-pendency was and ways it can manifest in life. The correlations she made between codependency and other problems such as depression, apathy, overeating, alcoholism, and physical health issues like diabetes and heartache were astounding to me. It became clear that codependency was a lifestyle, a deeply rooted issue from childhood.

I loved doing research, and I found that the term "codependency" had been around for a long time. In one article, I read that codependency forms when a child feels like a burden to her caregivers. The child feels an obligation to emotionally take care of her caregiver, hoping the parent will respond in a loving and caring way toward them. Children can't take care of themselves or their basic needs, making codependency a survival skill, a tactic used by children to maneuver the complexity of their parents in order to get their basic needs met in this world. Sadly, these traits become the normal way of life for the child when interacting with other people. The child learns that by doing things for others and pleasing them, people will eventually reciprocate.

I reflected on the articles and books I read for the rest of the night. The life I had been living was all I knew. How could I start over? As a child, I turned to God for help in times of need, and, boy, did I need Him now.

Geneva and I had just started our support group at church, and I was assigned to be one of the facilitators, but I realized I had to step down and be a participant. I had to stop caring for others and care for myself, but how? My career as a social worker was rooted in social services and helping people. I took pride in my skillset and felt I needed to use it everywhere. I knew this was a big change, and I had to search through my heart and mind and ask God to guide me through my healing process.

I started reading the twelve-step book at work the next day and doing the exercises. Learning to live by the twelve steps was helping me create a new foundation for the life of freedom ahead of me. The lesson plans for recovery were not easy. Many of the questions were intense and required me to take a deep self-inventory of who I was and how I showed up in the world. They awakened my insecurities. They unmasked the things I was trying to hide from myself and others. Admitting the answers to many of those questions meant admitting I had a problem. And I wasn't ready to do that.

It was Friday night, and I was ready to attend group. I had been reading about codependency and doing the exercises in the twelve-step book for two days. I was ready to participate in the support group. Instead of going to Joanne's church, I decided to attend one of the meetings at my church. I felt bad that I couldn't help Geneva as a facilitator like we'd planned, but I was glad she understood.

As I pulled up to the building, I saw about ten cars. "Wow, it's a full house tonight."

I got out of the car and saw Geneva and our other church friend, Roland. Roland had been in recovery for over fifteen years, and he was happy that our church had finally decided to incorporate a recovery program. He came up to me with open arms, smiling, showing all his teeth. "Amen, amen! Good to see you, Sister Taneshia."

I laughed. "Hey, Roland. I'm happy to see you, too. How are you?"

"They tell me the program works if you work it, sister, amen? So that's what I'm doing. Geneva told us you were no longer going to facilitate as planned. I was sad when I didn't see you, but Geneva and Janice are doing a good job. I have been praying for you, sister. I said to myself, Sister Taneshia must have realized she needs to take care of herself."

I looked at Roland, confused. What did he mean? How could Joanne, my therapist, and now even Roland see I needed help? "What, what do you mean?" I asked.

"Sister, if you're ready to hear the truth, let me know."

"I'm ready," I said with my hand on my hip."

"Taneshia, I have been knowing you for almost ten years now. You go around taking care and worrying about everyone but you. Anytime I ask how you're doing, you mention how your mama, daddy, best friend, and everybody else is doing. I asked about you, not them. That let me know that you didn't know how you were doing because you didn't know *you*. Now that you're taking time for yourself, it's only going to get easier. Do you have a therapist?"

I looked at him with tears in my eyes and gave him a hug. It was such a relief that someone else identified with my struggle and could put words to it when I couldn't. I didn't know any other way to be, and thinking of me first felt scary and confusing. I didn't know how. I tightened my arms around him and cried.

"Amen, sister. It's gonna be all right," he said holding me close. "Put your faith and trust in God, Taneshia. He will show you the way, but you first have to be ready. You taking time for you is the first step." He glanced inside my car and saw my candy wrappers and chips. He softly put his hand in mine and whispered, "And, sister, put the food down. Food will not help you. Snickers and Lays potato chips are not your friend. Only God can do something about the problems we have on this earth. Food is an addiction, Taneshia. I was addicted to crack cocaine for decades of my life. I know it when I see it. Come on in, and let's join the group."

I still couldn't speak. Tears drenched my face as I followed him inside.

When I came in, I looked around. I hadn't been to the group at my church.

I felt someone tap me on my shoulder. I turned around and saw Geneva.

"Taneshia! It's so good to see you! Grab some food if you want and have a seat. Just relax."

I smiled at her. "Thank you," I said.

As I glanced down at the lesson plan, I saw our first lesson was on denial. *What denial?* I thought. Everyone else was hurting me; what could I have been in denial about?

Taneshia, this whole thing makes no sense because you're not supposed to be here, girl. Go home! You have papers due and, not to mention, class tomorrow. You have done too much this week as is. First, Wednesday, you went to therapy, then you spent all day yesterday researching this codependency crap, and now you're here in the group? You are a professional mental health advocate and social worker. You help people who are here, you don't attend groups with them!

I was interrupted from my thoughts as Jane and Geneva started to lead group. "Hello, hello, and thank you, everyone for coming. You could have been anywhere else tonight, but you are here healing with us! Give yourself a round of applause!" Jane said.

Jane was so funny. She was my friend and sister in Christ. I admired how beautiful and confident she was. She encouraged me and advised me not to let my circumstances lead me down a path of destruction and pain. I was happy to see her helping Geneva with the group when I couldn't. I took my seat next to Roland and opened my twelve-step book.

"Thank you, Jane. Let us pray," Roland said.

We all took each other's hand at the table and bowed our heads.

"Heavenly Father, we want to say thank you, Lord, for allowing us to be together tonight. The devil had us in bondage all week, but we made it to your Kingdom, Lord. We ask that you cure us of our addictions and compulsive behaviors. Help us to see that all things work together when we put our trust in You. Lord, we are thankful for our leader Taneshia joining us tonight. Thank you, Lord, that she is loosening these chains of codependency and overeating. Thank you, Lord, for all those present tonight under the sound of my voice. We ask, Lord, that you bless this group. Let us all learn what we are in denial about so we can gain clarity and have peace. In the name of Your Son Jesus Christ, we pray. Amen."

"Amen," we all said.

I looked up, and there wasn't a dry eye in the room. Everyone was either crying or had been crying during prayer, including myself. I was shocked that Roland looked at me as a leader, even though I couldn't facilitate. It gave me courage to look at myself as a leader for going to therapy, accepting that I may be a codependent and getting the help I needed.

CHAPTER 5

DEPRESSION

While in group, I couldn't focus. I found that reading about denial triggered me. I refused to believe I was in denial. I dazed out for most of the group. The nice thing about participating and not facilitating was I didn't have to worry about keeping up with the lesson.

After group was over, I hopped into my car and decided to call Joanne and tell her about my accomplishment.

"Hey, girl! What you doing?"

"Hey, Taneshia! I'm surprised to hear your voice. Ms. I Gotta Go!"

We both laughed. "What you mean?"

"Taneshia, I know you like I know the back of my hand; you ain't slick! You just wanted to rush me off the phone on Wednesday 'cause you know I'm right! So go ahead and tell me all the research you did. I know you. I'm sure you stayed up half the night trying to convince yourself you're not codependent. Am I right?"

"What can I say? When you're right, you're right!" We both laughed. "I did, and you were right. I *am* codependent. One of the books I read even talked about how people have addictions to cope with the people pleasing that comes with codependency. Mine, of course, is food."

"Wow, okay. I see you, boo! Stepping up! Being honest with yourself. Yes, honey!"

We shared another laugh.

My line beeped with an incoming call. It was my cousin. He owed me money, and I wondered if he was calling to pay me back. I sure could've used it. "Joanne, let me call you back. This is my cousin."

"This late? What he want? Did you give him money again?"

"Yes, I did, but this is definitely the last time."

"Mm hm. I've heard that before. Okay, call me back, girl. I wanna hear more."

"Okay, Joanne. I want you to know I love you."

"I love you more, Ms. TJ Selfcare."

"Who is TJ Selfcare?" I asked.

"That's my new name for you. Taneshia Johnson is finally taking care of herself!"

"All right, now. I like that!" I said. We giggled as I ended the call with Joanne and clicked over to my cousin. "Hey, cuz. What's good?"

"I got bad news and good news," he started. "Good news is I have the money for you. Bad news is my daughter needs braces. You think I could pay you back next month?"

What? Who does that? Tell someone you have their money

then say you need it for something else? You were going to use that money to help pay your phone bill. If he doesn't give it to you, you'll have to use your credit card that you've already racked up!

"Okay, just keep the money. Listen, it's late and I have to go, okay? I'm getting ready to walk into my apartment. Talk to you later."

"Okay, I'm really sorry, Taneshia."

I hung up. I didn't want to hear more excuses from him. He had been doing this for years. It was almost like his daughters were mine. I walked into the house tired and sad. The small bit of joy I had gotten from going to group was zapped away in less than five minutes of being on the phone with my cousin. It was like people had power over my emotions, and I didn't like it.

I took a long, hot shower, put my pajamas on, and flipped through my twelve-step book. I reviewed the lesson plan again and looked over the twelve steps, reading them out loud. "Step one: Realize I am not God. I admit that I am powerless to control my tendency to do the wrong thing and my life has become unmanageable."

I finally started putting all the pieces together. I was beginning to realize I had created this world where I was helping everyone constantly and hurting myself in the process. The thought of it frightened me so badly that it made me cry. This was not the life God intended for me but the life I had created for myself because I was afraid to say no and set boundaries with people out of fear of being abandoned if I did. I had so many questions and concerns. If I had caused it, how could I end it? Would God help me? And if so, how could He break me free from the chains I used to shackle myself?

I flipped through the lesson plan and looked over the

questions. The first question read: "One: What area of your life is out of control or unmanageable?" If I had seen that question a few weeks ago, I would've said none, but stepping into this new reality where I was admitting to myself that I was a people pleaser, codependent, and an emotional eater, I knew better. My entire life had become unmanageable, and I needed God to help me. I put the twelve-step book on my desk and went to bed. My mind was crowded with information, and it all felt like too much.

I cried myself to sleep. I tried not to process each thought that seeped into my head, but I couldn't help it. I listened to each one and agreed. I had ruined the only thing I had going for myself. I was a counselor ... who had a therapist. I was a group facilitator ... who was now in a group herself. I felt like a complete failure.

I was so busy moping all week that I went to bed forgetting that the next day was Saturday. "Shit!" I said as I looked at the clock. I had spent another night of crying myself to sleep and forgot to set my alarm clock. It was 7:30 a.m., and class started at 8:45. I jumped out of bed, got into the shower, threw my clothes on, and jumped into my car. "Shit, shit, shit! I didn't do my paper! Oh, Lord!"

The drive that would normally take me forty-five minutes took thirty. I parked in the parking lot closest to the school and ran to class. It was nine a.m., and the teacher had barely started talking. I was so relieved.

"Don't worry; you good," my friend Ron said.

Ron was like my brother. He had my back in every class. He

was tired of school just like I was, but he was better at getting to class on time and finishing assignments.

"Ron, is that paper for research class due today or next week?"

"Nah, it's actually due next *month*. Taneshia, you okay?" he asked, rubbing my shoulder.

"Yeah, yeah, I'm good. I guess I wrote down the wrong date."

"You know me or one of the girls would've reminded you."

The girls were our friends, Lisa, Nikki, Tonya, and Angela. I was thankful to have such beautiful people in my circle of friends who texted me to remind me of due dates, let me borrow their books, and, most importantly, loved me when I didn't love myself.

"What you get on the last paper?" Ron asked.

"I got an A. Can you believe it?" I said, amazed that I had gotten an A on a paper I had done the night before. I guess I was smart.

"Hell yeah, you got an A! You the shit!" We laughed.

"Could you guys keep it down? I'm trying to learn," Nikki said with a smile. "Hey, girl!" she said to me. "I got you something." She pulled out a pair of bronze earrings that said Black Queen on them.

"Aw, thank you," I said. I started crying but quickly wiped my tears. Nikki was so sweet. She was like an older version of Joanne. They both saw such power and beauty in me. I couldn't understand why I couldn't see it in myself.

"Awww shit! Little TJ over here tearing up," Ron teased.

We chuckled as people started staring at us. We quickly quieted down and listened to the professor.

The professor spoke about depression. As he stated some of

the symptoms, I contemplated if that was something I struggled with. I was learning I struggled with so many things; what was one more problem? I glanced over the symptoms in my textbook as he lectured: overeating, not eating enough, lack of energy, sleeping too much or not enough, feeling hopeless, and losing interest in things you once enjoyed. For a moment, I zoned out and began reflecting on myself and how I had been feeling lately. Was it depression? I had been going to therapy, and my therapist never mentioned depression. She just talked about my self-worth, Shawn, and my dad. I was determined to find out more information.

"Girl, I thought we were never going to get out of that class," Angela said with a smile.

"I know. How many times can he wear the same pants over and over?" Lisa said.

"He been wearing those pants for the last two months. Either they not paying him enough or he nasty. One of the two," Ron added.

"Oh, Jesus! Y'all are too funny!" I said.

"Taneshia, so the next paper is due next month. Did you start yet?" Angela asked.

"Hell nah, she hasn't! And she thought it was due today!" Ron yelled.

Everyone looked at me. I smiled, happy they were looking out for me. "I'm walking to my car to go home and start researching now."

"All right! No waiting until the last minute like last time. Just because you got an A last time, doesn't mean you will again," Tonya said.

We all gave each other hugs, and everyone went their separate ways.

There was no traffic on the freeway, and I was able to drive without distractions. As I drove, I examined my life. I was thirty years old and had been feeling my mind and spirit changing for awhile. I was tired all the time. I lacked energy to enjoy activities and things I used to do regularly. When someone called or texted, I dreaded picking up the phone or calling back. *What do they want?* I'd think. *Don't they know I have things to do like lie in my bed, eat ice cream, cry, and try to figure out where my life went wrong?* It was true. I was likely depressed, but something inside me still didn't want to believe it. How could I be depressed when I had so much perseverance? According to the diagnosis, I shouldn't have been able to complete my homework, go to work every day, smile, and keep up with my life. I wanted more information.

I pulled up to my apartment complex and immediately ran to my room and found my Diagnosis Statistical Manual. The DSM book had all the diagnoses known in the world and broke down each mental health disorder into symptoms and treatment. If I was depressed, this book would help guide me to the next step. I searched and found a disorder called dysthymia, now known as persistent depression disorder. As I read through the criteria, I felt my face getting warm. Tears formed in my eyes. I had all the symptoms.

As I turned each page of the book, I soaked in all the information about the disorder: "This disorder is a long-term (chronic) form of depression. May cause loss of interest in normal daily activities, feelings of guilt, lack of productivity, low self-esteem, and overall feeling of inadequacy. Symptoms can last for years."

Years, I thought. *Have I been depressed for years and didn't realize it?*

As I continued to read more, I learned that, apparently, this form of depression was minor compared to major depressive disorder, which was much more severe. However, the danger in persistent depression disorder was that it was long-term and, therefore, could be easily overlooked as just feeling sad or having a melancholy mood. Prior to this year, I was a happy person. I enjoyed doing fun things with family and friends, and I loved life. Acknowledging that those feelings were no longer the same for me felt heavy.

My breaths became labored and tears began to fall. I sat on the edge of my bed and cried. I searched my room for more textbooks that might tell me I wasn't depressed, but I had to acknowledge my harsh reality—I was depressed, and I didn't know how to get out of it. I suddenly became angry with myself, my existence, and what I was experiencing. I opened a bottle of wine and stayed up all night researching YouTube videos and trying to get more clarification. I wanted to find something that told me this wasn't depression, that it was just a phase I was going through and it would soon end. I was hoping someone had beat this thing without medication and could give some feedback. Depression was something I counseled and educated people about, never something I thought I would face. I felt alone.

I felt myself spiraling out of control. I pulled up Shawn's Facebook account. Although there were no new pictures, I lashed out, yelling at his pictures as if he could hear me.

Sad R&B music played in the background. I'd had one too many glasses of wine. I just wanted to get drunk and forget this day existed, forget that I'd found out I was struggling with depression.

•——————•——————•

The week went by fast, and it was Wednesday again. Time to see Dr. Jones. It was about 5:15 p.m. when I saw my supervisor leaving the building. "Damn, what the hell is David still doing here? It's past five. He usually goes home at four," I whispered to myself. I tried to ignore him and go the other way, but it was too late. He had seen me coming out the front door.

"Taneshia, you were late again today. This is becoming a problem."

"I wasn't late today. I had a home visit with a client this morning," I said, angry that he was accusing me of being late. I did have a pattern of tardiness, but today wasn't one of those days.

"You emailed me at 8:07 a.m.; that's late. You were supposed to be here at eight a.m."

"No, I emailed you at 8:07 a.m. to let you know I had a home visit. I was already at the client's house. You can call her if you want."

David stepped back and took his glasses off. This was not a good sign. Normally, in black culture, when someone removed his glasses, it either meant he was about to attack with his mouth or his fists, and considering the fact that both David and I were black and had grown up in similar neighborhoods, I knew he knew what he was doing. Either way, I was tired of David and ready to knock him out if needed.

"Taneshia, I'm not going to go back and forth about this with you. Either come to work on time, or there will be consequences."

Consequences? Boy, bye! My coworker and I run this whole program while you sit on your ass! I'm helping homeless families find housing on a daily basis, and I'm being chastised for being late on a day that I wasn't late! Why am I standing here? I should just knock you out, go to jail, and be done with it. Then I wouldn't have to worry about anyone. I wouldn't be able to help anyone. I could just be free and by myself!

"I have to go. Good day, David." I walked away quickly, headed to my car. It was 5:30 p.m. I was late for therapy.

Why didn't you say anything, fool? There you go again! You let this man get away with murder!

I didn't have time to go back and forth with my negative thoughts. I needed therapy today, and I was running late.

As I sped down the street, I thought about questions I wanted to ask Dr. Jones about depression. There had to be some kind of test or something she could give me to prove that my feelings about being depressed weren't true.

"Good afternoon, Taneshia," Dr. Jones said when I arrived.

"Hi, I'm so sorry I'm late. My supervisor held me up."

"It's okay. I have some extra time today to give you. We have some things to talk about."

I sat, reclined the seat, and looked at her from the sides of my eyes. *Things to talk about? What is she talking about?* "Well, it's funny you mention that because I want to talk to you about depression," I said.

"Really. Mm hm. This is interesting. Share more."

"Why is it interesting? Do you feel I'm depressed?" My voice

72

had elevated and my neck moved side to side as I spoke. I knew this woman was not about to sit there and tell me she had been writing in her notes that I was depressed and didn't bother to tell me.

"Taneshia, I need you to breathe. Let's breathe together."

We both inhaled and exhaled deeply twice.

"How do you feel?" she asked.

I opened my eyes to tears coming down my face. I pulled some tissue from the box next to me. "I feel like weights are attached to my ankles. Like every move I try to make, I'm either stagnant or derailed. The feeling lasts for days sometimes. Some mornings, it takes me at least thirty to forty-five minutes just to decide if I should get out of my bed. I often contemplate if it's even worth it. I struggle to do everything, go to work, wash dishes, do laundry ... The only thing that's important to me is finding ways to lie in bed and never go anywhere or do anything for anyone again."

Wow, Taneshia, you are just spilling all the beans today! Well, since you're telling her everything, might as well tell her you hate your job. When was the last time you actually enjoyed helping your clients? Even better, when was the last time you went out with your friends? You remember them, right, the people you're ignoring who care about you? Taneshia, you're ruining your future. How are you going to tell your mom this? All her years of sacrifice gone to waste. Please don't tell your dad. This is an embarrassment to your whole family.

I cried freely. Dr. Jones gave me some time to reflect.

"Taneshia, let's take a pause. May I share my thoughts?"

"Okay."

"I was going to share with you today that based on our

sessions, you do demonstrate signs of general anxiety and moderate levels of depression. I believe both your anxiety and your depression are deeply rooted in your codependency traits. I'm sure you're wondering what I mean by this, so let me take a minute to explain."

I sat upright, eager to hear. A part of me felt relieved that she was giving me a diagnosis because I knew I could get better; I just needed someone to help me.

"You love both your parents very much, is this correct?"

"Yes, it is."

"Okay, well, we all know that parenting does not come with a handbook. Many children who are raised in single-parent homes tend to think they're little adults. They think taking care of their caregivers will relieve stress from their parents so they can love and nurture them. Sadly, this creates a dynamic where the child grows up feeling like they're responsible for people around them. Taking care of your parent emotionally or anyone else was not your job as a child, nor is it now as an adult. How does all this sound so far?"

"It sounds accurate. I've been reading about codependency and read the same thing, but why am I depressed or have anxiety?"

"Yes, so your anxiety traits were made clear to me based on your constant body movements during session and your negative thought patterns. You've mentioned that you feel like your thoughts are voices. Do you *hear* the thoughts or think them?"

"I think them, but my thoughts feel so loud in my head."

"Many people with anxiety and depression struggle with negative self-talk. It's common. The proper term for it is intrusive thoughts. Do you feel they control you?"

"No, but they put me down."

"Put you down how? Say more."

"The things they say to me make me feel bad. My thoughts tell me I'm nothing, that people don't really love me and everything I'm doing is senseless."

"Mmm. I see. Do you think people love you?"

"Yes."

"Great. Let's name some. Who are some of the people who love you?"

I was shocked that she wanted me to name them on the spot, but I did. "Well, my mom and dad, of course, and my best friend, Diane. Really, all my friends. I have some really great friends," I said, smiling. "My grad school friends are awesome. They have my back all the time, make sure I never miss a session. My family in Georgia and Florida care about me, my church family. Oh, I can't forget about my support group family. We send each other inspirational texts throughout the week."

Dr. Jones and I both smiled. "Wow! Taneshia, that is a lot of people. Out of this group of people, who do you feel loves you the most?"

"My mom, dad, and best friend, Diane."

"Tell me a little about your mother."

"My mother was strict and firm with me growing up. She had an authoritative parenting style; however, she loved me and sacrificed herself to raise me."

"So, even though your relationship with your dad isn't as strong as you would like and your mother was strict, you believe they both love you the most?"

"Oh, yeah!" I said, throwing my hand up. "Without a shadow of a doubt. My mom worked two jobs to make sure

I had the best in life. She is a huge provider. She is the reason I have the discipline and direction I have in life now. My dad makes it a point to talk to me two to three times a week. We don't talk long, but he tells me he loves me each time, and, lately, we talk more in depth. Our relationship is growing, I have plans to see him soon. He loves me. There is no doubt about that, and I love him and my mother very much."

"I see. So it sounds like your thoughts are not true when they tell you people don't love you."

I paused, starting to cry again. I grabbed more tissue. "Yeah, they're wrong. How do I stop them, Dr. Jones?" I asked, pleading with her to help me.

"Taneshia, I thought you'd never ask." We both chuckled as she pulled out some graphs. She gave me a form labeled Daily Affirmations. "Taneshia, you have a little homework for next session. For the next seven days, I want you to write down five affirmations about yourself. You should have thirty-five by the next time I see you. I want you to start with 'I am.' For example: I am light, I am beautiful, I am worthy, I am love, etc. Do you think you can do that?" she asked with a smile.

"Yes, yes I can."

We talked further about the affirmations, and Dr. Jones explained their importance and the impact they can have on my outlook on life. At this point, I was willing to try anything to reclaim normalcy, so I figured it was worth a shot.

"Okay. We have run out of time. How do you feel?"

"I feel a little better."

"Okay. Know that things will get better." We both stood and shook hands. "I'll see you next week. Take care." She closed the door.

I walked out of the session with my intrusive thoughts on overload. They were shooting through my mind like fire crackers on the Fourth of July. As I walked to my car, I saw the cupcake shop on Telegraph I had gone to before. I was just a few blocks away. I went into the bakery and got four cupcakes. Before I got to my car, two of them were gone.

Taneshia, are you really eating cupcakes in the cold? And why four cupcakes? You don't think you're going overboard right now? What is happening to you?

I got into the car and placed the cupcake container next to me. I picked another one up and began to eat it. I examined my face in the rearview mirror. I saw myself trying to eat the pain away. I put the cupcake down, wiped the frosting off my mouth, and began to cry. Psalms 42:3 (NIV) states, "My tears have been my food day and night, while they continually say unto me, 'Where is your God.'" After years of sitting in church, I was growing to understand what that verse meant. I had cried more in these last weeks than I had in a lifetime. Every time I tried to pray, tears swelled in my eyes, and all I could do was cry out to God, hoping He could understand my thoughts and take the pain away.

I was broken, and trying to function in dysfunction wasn't working for me. Moving forward and being perseverant was all I knew how to do. I didn't know how to stop or even pause. I grew up concluding that life was going to be hard. There would be hardships, but I would be ready for them and keep moving. I felt in my heart I needed to stop. I needed to find a way to pull myself together, but I couldn't. I hadn't processed the idea of being codependent yet, but here I was with another issue to work on—depression and anxiety. My recovery from codependency had become a requirement, but it felt hard to break this code-pendent lifestyle I had created because everything I did was built on what I did for others: my job as a social worker, how I interacted with family and friends, and how I presented myself to the world. My arms were always open to everyone, hoping they'd see how great I was and they'd love me. I thought by be-ing there for others, they would be there for me. What I found was people used me, and others didn't understand the level of sacrifice I was making to be there for them, so they didn't appreciate my support the way I wanted them to. I often didn't get the credit I deserved, even when I had done the work. My job was a prime example. David never praised me for the great job I was doing nor for staying late without getting paid. All he cared about was the fact that I was ten or fifteen minutes late to work. My coworker was constantly late, even more than I was. I regularly met with his clients and mine, and I barely got a thank you for that. My cousin didn't care that I was strug-gling financially; all he thought about was himself. Because I had given him money in the past and he knew I had no kids, I allowed him to make me his personal ATM.

Now, living as a recovering codependent who struggled with depression *and* anxiety, I had to figure out what I needed. That was like a whole new world that felt too hard for me, but I trusted Dr. Jones, and, most importantly, I trusted that God had sent her to help me learn how to live the life He had for me.

I got home that night and started writing my affirmations. It felt weird to think about myself and all the things I am. My focus had always been on others. I knew how to empower other people. I had been trained in my profession, and I loved to share with others how amazing and beautiful they were; however, I didn't know how to do it for myself.

I sat on the edge of my bed and started writing:

"I am love."

Okay that's one.

"I am successful."

That's two.

"I am beautiful."

"I am giving."

"I am loving."

"I am kind."

"I am intelligent."

"I am worthy of love."

Wow, look at all these "I am" statements. I looked over my notebook paper, amazed that I had just written all those affirmations. I smiled, laid my notebook on my desk, and said my prayers.

"Dear God, I guess this is the breakthrough you knew would happen. I don't know what she is doing, but it feels good. Today, she had me reflect on all the people who love me. I guess I'm crazy, I don't know. I always tend to have so many negative thoughts, Lord. I just want them to end. Please help me. Help me see myself as You and everyone else see me. Amen." I pulled the sheet over my legs and arms and stared out the window. As I looked up at the stars, I smiled. For once in a long time, I wasn't crying myself to sleep, and it felt good.

———◆———

It was Friday afternoon. My work colleagues and I were preparing for our weekly staff meeting. The meetings were boring.

David lacked the qualifications to be a supervisor and often leaned on my coworkers and me to complete his data work and make him look good. Because of my lack of drive for the job and current mood, I was seeking other alternatives for work. I had put in a few applications, but no one had contacted me yet.

As my coworkers and I sat in the meeting, I suddenly had to use the restroom. I had been holding it for the last ten minutes and didn't want to damage my bladder just to hear the same thing my supervisor had previously stated in emails and phone calls that week.

When I got up to go, he frowned and asked, "Where are you going? We're in a meeting."

"I have to use the restroom. I'll be back," I responded, confused. What was this? I couldn't go to the bathroom? The man was crazy. I went to the bathroom and took a few minutes to decompress before I went back to the meeting. I ran my fingers through my wig, remembering when I used to have full, curly hair. Stress had thinned my hair and wigs had become my best friend. I glanced down at my hands. They were shaky, and my heart was fluttering. I didn't know what was going on. I quickly remembered Dr. Jones had said this was a sign of my anxiety, but I didn't know how the two connected.

I grabbed some water from the vending machine and walked back. "Lord, keep my heart from flying out of my chest during this meeting," I said quietly. I wished I had some candy, but water was going to have to do.

When I came back, all my coworkers' heads were down. Some were on their phones and others seemed to be meditating. I wondered why the meeting hadn't started.

"We've been waiting for you to return," David said with

the same grimace he had when I'd left. "Now, let's talk about some things I am no longer going to accept from my staff. You all walk around as if other supervisors and managers don't talk to me about what is going on. If this is going to work, we must act as a unit. I don't tolerate any foolishness. I believe gossip and foolishness is like cancer. It spreads and destroys the whole team, and before it does, I will cut it out."

What the hell was he talking about? He was known for making analogies that made no sense to anyone but him. I glanced around the table and noticed that everyone either had their heads down or was in a daze. I looked back at David and, to my surprise, he was looking directly at me.

It reminded me of being in a classroom while the teacher reprimanded a student in front of her peers. But what had I done? I had been on time for work since our last altercation that week. Yes, I was looking for another job but had never shared that with anyone in the agency. If anything, my coworkers were the ones asking around about jobs and applying for others within the agency. So why was all the focus on me?

Suddenly, he slapped the table. I thought I was dreaming, but it was more like a nightmare happening right before my eyes. "You need to respect me!" he yelled. "You think people like you? They don't like you! They don't care anything about you. Respect me! I am your supervisor!"

I was in a daze. I didn't know what to say. It was almost like he knew the thoughts in my head and was confirming them in front of everyone. I looked at one of my coworkers, who was more like a sister, and she stared back at me, shaking her head. We both figured he was talking about us, but we didn't understand what had happened. Was this about me being late? And if so, why not talk to me privately? We all sat there in silence shocked by his response.

"I don't understand what's happening. Is this because of something I did?" I asked, pointing at myself.

"I'm not going to call anyone out in front of people, but at the same time, don't act like you don't know what I'm talking about."

I was confused. I glanced at the clock and saw it was past five p.m.

"Well, it's 5:05, and I'm not going to hold you all up any longer. My message to everyone is to stay focused on the job and keep what happens in our department between us. Have a good weekend." And just like that, David got up from the table, pulled out his car keys, and started walking to the parking lot.

After the meeting, I went to my car to cry. My car had been a sacred space for my tears. But my tears turned into rage. I watched as everyone drove off for the weekend. My coworker called me, but I didn't answer the phone. I just stared at the screen. I dazed out staring at the leaves on the tree next to me. In my mind, David was another person that was using me and felt he could talk to me any kind of way because he knew I wouldn't do anything. I was tired, tired of people thinking they could walk over me, ask me for help all the time and expect me to just drop everything. I realized that before I had gone to the support group, that was my life—people pleasing, catering to other people, and allowing people to talk to me *and* treat me badly.

I wanted David to pay for what he did to me this time.

I heard my thoughts talking to me again. *What happened now? I can't believe you just sat there and let him talk to us like that. You should do something. Do something, Taneshia! My goodness. All you do is cry. You're so weak. You can add this to the list. Codependent, depressed, anxious, and weak.*

I wasn't weak. I was strong. I had come from a line of people with the ability to turn malicious if necessary. I was growing angry. As I wiped my tears, I thought of ways to get him back. I had a list of friends from my old neighborhood who would come beat him up, but how could I get away with it without getting fired or going to jail? Maybe going to his house would be best. Another thought popped into my head: *Maybe I can unscrew the nails to his chair in his office, and the next time he sits down, he'll fall.* Hopefully, he'd break a leg, arm, or, if I was lucky, both. That would force him to go on leave from work for a while, giving me a break from him. That was a better idea. I found myself smiling so hard my cheeks hurt. It was a perfect plan.

As I pondered on the thought, I grew disappointed in myself. Was this what I had come to? A malicious, passive aggressive person who found comfort in plotting on ways to hurt other people? I couldn't believe it. I was allowing my negative thoughts to control my actions and almost make me risk my job and going to jail. It was crazy.

I soon realized the awareness I had about what I was planning was based on who I was. Yes, I was codependent, I had allowed people to use me, and I wanted to play the victim in all areas of my life, yet my harsh reality was that everyone who had hurt me was able to do so because I allowed it. I was in control.

So, there I was sitting in my car, having an epiphany and a newfound understanding of my pathology. I tried to figure out what my next steps should be. I had grown tired of trying to piece things together on my own and decided to do what I knew best: talk to God.

I closed my eyes and prayed. "Dear Lord, here I am again. I can't believe I'm really sitting here thinking of ways to harm someone. Lord, I don't want to be this kind of person. I want to learn to stand up for myself, say no, and set boundaries with people. I shouldn't have allowed David to walk to his car until he was clearer with me, and I should've told him how I feel. I am one of his best employees, God! Clients rave about me to him all the time. Why can't he see it? Why is he always on my back? Lord, please. Please come into this space. Come into my heart and show me how to break these codependent chains. In the name of Your Son, Jesus Christ, I pray. Amen."

I felt His presence with me. It was comforting. I had forgotten how healing prayer was for me. I sat in silence for about fifteen minutes, cried, and wrote my five affirmations for the day. The Lord was there with me, and I knew things were going to get better.

CHAPTER 6

LEARNING TO PRAY WHEN BEING DIAGNOSED

"Yes, today is Wednesday!" I hopped out of bed in amazement. Wednesday had become my favorite day of the week. I was ready to go to work and quickly end the day so I could go to therapy. It actually felt good to know I was struggling with depression and anxiety. Finally, things made sense. No wonder I didn't have any energy, always felt lethargic, and had no desire to do anything.

I began to get ready. I was tired of throwing on sweats and mix-matched shoes. I found a cute blue dress in the closet and my favorite sandals to match. I had not been wearing colors for a while. It felt good to dress up. I knocked on my mom's door, and, to my surprise, she was already up also getting ready for work.

"Good morning, Mookie. Look at you, already up and

going. I'll see you tonight. Do you have any late appointments?" she asked.

"No, not today. I have therapy."

"Oh, okay. Well, I'll see you when you get home. Love you."

"Okay, I love you, too," I said and closed her bedroom door.

Dr. Jones was right. The thoughts in my head were wrong; my mom did love me. I hopped into the car and started the engine. I picked up the phone to call my dad.

"Is this my beautiful daughter, Taneshia Johnson?" my dad said.

I always laughed when he said that. "Yes, of course, it's me, Dad. How are you?" We both laughed.

"I'm doing all right, daughter. How are you?"

"I'm okay. I found a therapist."

"Oh, wow! Really? Why do you think you need that?"

"Well, I've been struggling lately to stay on top of things, and I talk to my clients about going to therapy all the time. I figure I need to go, too."

"I see. Hey, well, I love you. I'm here, and let me know what she says. I pray it's helpful to you."

Wow! I was in shock. A positive comment from my dad about therapy, and he had offered to listen. "Okay," I said. "I will. I love you, Dad."

"I love you, too, Taneshia. Bye bye."

I drove to work smiling the whole way. I realized I had assumed my parents didn't care about what I was going through. It was another intrusive thought that had entered my mind based on past experiences. I started to wonder what other untrue negative messages I had told myself. Yes, there were times when people did treat me unfairly, but I believed everyone was treating me unfairly all the time. But that was my anxiety, not reality. I was thankful for Dr. Jones and thankful to God for sending her. I was relieved to finally be figuring things out and gaining control over my thoughts and emotions.

Work was over in a flash. I jetted out and saw David walking to his car, so I decided to cross to the next street. I didn't have time for his petty bull. I got into my car and started down the street. Every light I went through was green, and I got to Dr. Jones's office in less than ten minutes. There was a parking spot right in front. "Wow! Parking again. This is great!" I was so happy to be making it somewhere on time. It meant a lot to know that I was putting my needs first, not scheduling late appointments with clients, not being on the phone for hours with my friends and family but carving out an hour every week just for me. It was a huge accomplishment.

I walked into her office on a cloud. This was session six, and I had learned so much about myself already. I looked forward to sharing the epiphany I'd had and gaining her insight on next steps as well as showing her my affirmations for the week.

"Hi, Taneshia! Welcome. So good to see you," she said.

"Hi, Dr. Jones. Good to see you, too." I sat in the recliner, dropped my purse, and got ready to dive into the session.

"Taneshia, I know you have the affirmations I suggested for you to do, so let's start with those."

I pulled out my list and showed her.

"Wow, very impressive! You actually have fifty here."

I smiled, proud of myself and happy she'd noticed there were more than the required thirty-five.

She reviewed the list, occasionally glancing at me and smiling. "So how did it feel to write these out? You have some amazing affirmations here, Taneshia. My favorite is 'I am unstoppable.'"

"It felt weird at first. I don't think I have ever completely focused on me before, but after a couple of days, it got easy, and I started to look forward to it. My supervisor banged on the table during a meeting with no real reason. I was so angry. Writing the affirmations afterward helped me remember who I am and not react in the way I had contemplated reacting."

Dr. Jones starting writing. "Mmm. I see. Say more about that."

"I was just so mad. I couldn't really focus on anything except how mad I was and what I could do to feel better."

"I see, and the affirmations reminded you of who you are?"

"Yes, they did. It was a life saver, too," I said laughing and remembering the crazy thoughts I'd had in my car.

"Taneshia, I'm curious to know if we can talk about the list of people you named last week who love you."

"Okay."

"Last week was the first time you mentioned Diane. You said she's your best friend. Tell me a little bit about her."

"Um, okay. I have no idea where to start because Diane has been my friend since I was five years old."

"Wow! This has been a long friendship. Well, let's see," she said, tapping her pen against her notebook. "Why don't you start by explaining the first incident that showed you Diane loved you."

I put my head down. To share that story, I would have to tell her I was diabetic. I didn't like telling people I was diabetic. I wasn't ashamed of it, but I knew if others knew, they would wonder why I had such horrible eating habits. One of the reasons Joanne was always on me about overeating was because she knew I was diabetic. The questions would come about why I didn't take care of my health, and I always struggled to find an explanation. I loved food and had just discovered I was a food addict. I didn't know how to explain all that to people; I was just understanding it myself.

"Well, I got really sick when I was sixteen years old, and I was in the hospital."

"Mm hm. I am sorry to hear that, Taneshia. May I ask you to elaborate if you feel comfortable?"

I knew where this was going, so I just blurted it out. "I'm a type 2 diabetic."

Dr. Jones looked at me and paused. "Oh. You never mentioned this before, right? Or did I miss this?"

"No, I never mentioned it. I usually don't."

"May I ask why?"

"It draws too much attention, and it's not a good memory for me."

"Mm hm. I see. Well, it sounds like that moment was somewhat special because you and Diane's friendship got closer. Is that fair to say?"

"Yeah. Diane has always been there for me. There have been times when I let her down. She didn't share a lot about how she felt when we were teenagers, so I monopolized our conversations. Thinking about how selfish I was still makes me cry sometimes. She and I have talked about it, and I apologized. She forgave me, and now things are great between us. I make it a point to give her space to share how she's doing before I tell her how I'm doing."

"Taneshia, that is great. I'm proud of you for acknowledging what was happening in your friendship with her. That says a lot about how you feel about her to make a change like that. Is it okay if we talk a little bit about your diabetes incident in the hospital and what led to it?"

"Sure, okay." I cleared my throat.

———————•———————

I was sixteen years old. I had been feeling sick for two months. I was constantly going to the bathroom and always thirsty. I had concluded that I was going to the restroom because I was drinking so much water and juice. I couldn't understand why I was thirsty, but I tried my best not to worry about it.

I worked part-time at Burger King in the Fillmore district of San Francisco. I went to work one day and could barely stand up. I figured I was sick, so I ate a salad and drank orange juice. I was in love with Burger King's Hershey chocolate pies and couldn't resist them, so I enjoyed one for dessert.

I ate my lunch as normal and went back to work. As I cleaned the restroom, I started feeling nauseated. Cleaning the bathrooms always made me feel sick, but this was different. My stomach was flipping inside my body. I suddenly threw up my entire lunch and was looking at it in the toilet. I didn't know what was going on. I sat on the toilet for ten minutes and cried, wondering what was wrong with me.

When I realized how long I had been gone, I rushed back to the register and worked the rest of the night. As I walked home, I felt tired and weak. My body felt lethargic, and I had no energy. When I got home, my great-aunt could tell I wasn't feeling well. She wanted me to call my mother. I called her and told her I didn't feel good. I gave her my symptoms, and she told me it sounded like the flu. She asked me to lie down until she got home.

Days passed, and I still didn't feel well. I was throwing up more and using the bathroom every five minutes. It was summer and school was out, but I still had to call out from work. As I lay in bed, I felt worse and worse. My head hurt, and it felt like rocks were weighing my body down. I had to find a way to the hospital. It was late in the day when I finally decided to go. I notified my mom and went to the bus stop.

As I sat outside waiting on the bus, my body felt increasingly weaker. I couldn't sit there anymore. I called my best friend, Diane, and asked if she and her mom could take me to the hospital. They showed up in fifteen minutes and took me. After being there for almost an hour, I spoke with a nurse. She ran tests on my urine and blood and revealed that I was diabetic. I didn't know what that meant. The doctor kept telling me my blood sugar was high. I asked myself, *What is that, and what did I do to deserve it?* Was this happening because I hadn't been praying? Was it punishment from God?

Diane and her mother left, and I was checked into the hospital. Nurses came into the room and immediately helped me onto a hospital bed. They rolled me to the intensive care unit. When I got there, they inserted multiple needles into my body.

As the nurses searched to find veins in my arms, I began to panic. *What's happening? How did I get this? Oh no! What about work and school? Am I dying?* I told myself things were fine. I would just be there overnight and go home in the morning.

"I have to go to the bathroom," I said.

"Honey, you can't go now. You're already hooked up to the blood pressure and insulin machine. Can you hold it?"

"No, I said I have to go."

As she walked away, I tried to figure out how to get out of the bed, but I couldn't. I was chained to the bed by various machines. I had no idea what they were for.

The nurse came back and placed a bedpan beneath me and told me to urinate inside the pan. I started to cry. She rubbed my shoulder and held my hand. She said some words, but I couldn't hear her because my tears and thoughts had consumed me.

I woke up the next morning hoping I'd had a nightmare. Sadly, I found that being in the hospital, diagnosed as a diabetic was my new reality. My mom was standing by my side. She told me everything would be okay, but in her eyes, I saw doubt.

After the doctors came in and explained what diabetes was and how to treat it, my mom had to go back to work. She gave me a kiss on the cheek and walked out. I saw her break down and cry outside my room. My mother rarely cried. I knew this "diabetes" thing was the end of me.

As I sat on my hospital bed, I tried to determine what I had done to get diabetes. *Have I done something to show God I wasn't worthy?* I felt abandoned and confused. I couldn't understand why, at only sixteen years of age, I had developed an incurable disease that would change my life.

I was in the hospital for four days. My mom worked on the fifth floor of the hospital and came to see me on her lunch break and after her shift. Diane also came up to the hospital and spent a day with me, but for most of the time, I was alone. I lay in my bed letting my tears fall from the sides of my eyes and saturate my pillow. Occasionally, the daytime nurse came in and held my hand and tried to make me laugh, but I was depressed and disappointed, and it was likely written on my face. Multiple doctors and nurses came in to explain to me what diabetes was, how to treat it, and they did their best to encourage me, but it didn't matter. I felt like God had left me. Why did I have this disease? What had I done? None of it made sense to me, no matter how many ways I tried to figure it out in my head.

Every two hours, a nurse came in and pricked my finger to test my blood sugar and check my vitals. There were three IVs: one for insulin, one for potassium, and another that administered electrolytes and other fluids my body needed.

The day before I was to be released, I cried silent tears while gazing out the window. I heard my door open. It was the doctor and my mom with an unfamiliar woman. I wiped my tears, hoping my eyes didn't look red or puffy. My mom had always taught me to be strong during times like this, and I didn't want her to see me crying.

"Hi, Taneshia," the doctor said in a solemn tone. "I'm Dr. Greenspan. I've been assigned as your release doctor. I know you've been here a long time, and you're ready to go home, but there's one last person I need to introduce you to."

The woman shook my hand. When she told me she was a nutritionist, I assumed she was going to tell me how fat I was and how my weight had contributed to my diabetes. My thoughts said, *Well, you are overweight, dark, and ugly, and now you have diabetes.* As I listened to the thoughts, I glanced around the room, surveying the blood pressure machine and heart monitor attached to me. The thought was right. I *was* ugly, overweight, and now I was sick. I was all alone. Even God had decided to abandon me. For so long, I had struggled with accepting myself. Getting diabetes felt like a punishment, but I didn't understand what I had done.

I looked at my mother sitting in a chair next to me. She looked scared. I had never seen that expression before. We had survived near homelessness, living in a one-bedroom apartment with my aunt, and many other hardships. We had been through the fire, and my mother had been through even more than I had. So to see her scared made me pay attention and face the harsh reality that I was really sick.

The nutritionist shared some information about diabetes and foods to avoid, and the doctor provided information about how to use my new blood sugar meter and inject insulin shots. The first time I pricked my finger to check my blood sugar, it hurt badly. My fingers hurt for ten to fifteen minutes afterwards. Sometimes, when the nurses left, I sat on the side of my bed, held my fingers, and cried. Looking at the blood sugar meter and insulin valves made me feel overwhelmed. I became anxious, worried that I would give myself too much insulin or not enough.

Release time was quickly approaching, and I only had a day to learn how to do everything before I was on my own. I didn't know anyone who had diabetes at my age. This was the first time I'd received a diagnosis I didn't know anything about and knew no one to ask.

As time went on, I learned more about diabetes. I was told that exercise and taking insulin could help me. I was overweight as a teenager. When I was diagnosed, I weighed 250 pounds. The doctors wanted me to lose weight. Because I was only sixteen years old, losing weight seemed to be the best solution. However, food was my comfort. I ate every time I felt any emotion: happiness, sadness, anger, etc. I didn't know how to endure life without food. My mom was working two jobs to provide for us. I was working part-time and my great-aunt, who was also raising me, had cervical cancer. It was an overload of situations that required me to be focused and present. If I couldn't eat, what was I going to do?

Diabetes had thrown a rod into my life, and I didn't know how to handle it.

My mother prepared healthy meals and encouraged me to exercise. After about a year, I lost thirty pounds. I was thankful to God. No more injecting myself with needles. It felt like such a blessing. I occasionally ate junk food, but God was with me. Because I had lost so much weight, my diabetes wasn't active. I could eat anything I wanted as long as I worked out. I realized God had answered my prayer. When doctors diagnosed me with a disease I couldn't overcome, I overcame it with the help of God.

———————

"Wow, it felt really good to tell you that story in its entirety! I have never shared it before," I said.

"Taneshia," she paused, "that is an amazing story. Let's sum up some of the things you said and connect them to the self-work you're doing now. What do you think about that?"

"Yes, please," I said, folding my hands and getting comfortable in the recliner.

"I want to start by saying you are a woman who is filled with power and capable of achieving anything. Going through something so traumatic at the age of sixteen is not easy. I know adults who were devastated when they were diagnosed with diabetes. So kudos to you on that, my dear!" she said, smiling. "Secondly, based on your story, I'm curious to know if you were suspicious that your love for food was an addiction even back then."

"It's funny you say that because I was, slightly. I didn't really know what an addiction was at sixteen, but I was suspicious that my eating habits seemed to be much different than my friends'."

"I see. Another thing I heard was how supportive your mother was during that process."

"Yes, she was. I lost thirty pounds because of my mother. She stayed on me!"

"Yeah, she did, while she worked two jobs, correct?"

"Yes, yes, she did."

"That's definitely love and dedication. And lastly, it sounds like you struggled with being diagnosed with diabetes, and ..." Dr. Jones paused and removed her glasses, "I wonder how you feel about being diagnosed with depression and general anxiety." She gave me a sympathetic look.

I grabbed a tissue and put my head down.

"Taneshia, we have about ten minutes left, but I want to take some time to really talk about how you feel. I think living as a codependent kept you safe in a lot of ways because it took the mirror off you and put it on other people. You didn't have to accept that you had a chronic disease and needed to take care of yourself, and you didn't have to accept that the relationships you desired with your mother and father were not there. Your mother had valid reasons for not being able to spend time with you. I am not condoning it; I am simply relaying to you what you have told me, and with your father living in a different state, it definitely wasn't feasible for him to be present for you in the way you may have desired him to be, like when eating dinner, teaching you to drive, going on walks, etc."

I let my tears freely pour from my eyes and stain my pants.

"Taneshia, I think one of the reasons you show a lot of sadness is because you did such a great job of pushing these memories down, and you didn't allow Little Taneshia to grieve her childhood experiences."

I looked up at her, confused. "Little Taneshia? Who is that?"

Dr. Jones leaned over and grabbed my hand. That's you, sweetie. The person who shows up to session is Little Taneshia. She didn't have a voice when you were younger, but here, she does, and she is very sad. She missed her parents growing up, and she was devastated when she found out she had diabetes. She needed someone, but she told herself she had no one. And maybe she didn't, but Adult Taneshia, which is you now, has done a great job in changing that narrative. Look at all the people you've named off who love you. You have created the relationship you wanted as a child with both of your parents now. Taneshia, your resiliency is astonishing. Do you see how amazing you are to have overcome all those obstacles and achieve so much? You are a soon-to-be master-level social worker, and you're a compassionate, giving, loyal, beautiful young woman who is loved by many people."

I felt like a spirit had taken over my body. I reached over and hugged Dr. Jones, and, to my surprise, she held me back. I put my head on her shoulder and cried.

"Let it out, Taneshia. It's okay. This is thirty years of tears. Take as long as you need." She rubbed my upper shoulder.

After a few minutes, I pulled away and smiled at her. "Thank you." I sat back in the recliner and grabbed more tissue next to me.

"You're welcome." She put her glasses back on and smiled.

"Normally, I wouldn't do that with a patient, but I could tell you needed it. How do you feel?"

"I feel lighter, like I really did just release a load of pain."

"Good. You have more homework. Are you ready?" Dr. Jones clapped her hands.

"Yeah, I am."

"Okay, I want you to find a picture of yourself as a child. It should be an image of you during a time you can remember feeling sad or unloved. Tell the picture that you love her and then apologize to her for not giving her a voice. Promise her that you will take care of her and get her needs met in ways that will not hurt you now."

"What? I'm confused."

"Okay, let me give you an example. Little Taneshia used food as a way to soothe the pain of her childhood experiences, but Adult Taneshia has diabetes and can't do that anymore. Am I making sense?"

"Oh, okay. I get it now. So another example would be Little Taneshia didn't tell people how she felt and developed passive aggressive behaviors to get what she wanted. So Adult Taneshia will work on being assertive and telling people how she feels in the moment. Is that right?"

Dr. Jones clapped again. "Yes, yes, yes! That is beautiful! Okay, so do that between now and next Wednesday, okay?"

"Okay."

Dr. Jones hugged me this time instead of shaking my hand. "See you next week."

———•———

A few days passed, and it was Saturday. After class, I

grabbed a drink with Nikki. Nikki had a ray of light around her that shined bright like a diamond. During the first week of class, we were told we would need to complete assignments weekly, could only miss three classes a semester, and we had to work for free at an organization of our choice. Looking back, I guess my anxiety had caused me to panic. I stepped outside of class, hands shaking, walking frantically down the hallway. Nikki came and held my hand and reminded me to have faith and hope and know that everything would be okay. It was so comforting. I knew God had sent her to be my friend and sister. Ever since then, she and I were close. I was close with all my friends in grad school.

"Whoah, girl! Can you say exhausted? Taneshia, I feel like we've been in school forever, girl!" Nikki said as we walked into the restaurant.

"I know. It's crazy, girl. Between working my crazy job, my internship, and dealing with life, it feels like too much, girl." We both nodded.

"So what's been going on, babe?" she said, putting her arm over my shoulder.

"Girl, where do I start? Ugh. Let's get a drink first, girl."

We immediately found a table. The place was a little hole-in-the-wall Mexican spot, but they had strong drinks and good food. As we took our jackets off and got comfortable, we called the waiter over.

"Hi, yes, may I order the chicken wings, a beef taco, and a strawberry mojito?" I had been watching my food intake for the last couple of weeks, and I was happy to be ordering a drink. I felt I deserved it.

"Hi, how are you? My name is Nikki. What's your name?" Nikki said.

"Derrick," the waiter said, laughing and glancing over Nikki. She was 5'6", curvy with long blonde locs and caramel skin. Her energy was magnetic, and she had a confidence I admired.

"I would like to order the chicken empanadas, and what drink do you recommend?" she asked with a smile.

"I think the peach mojito is my first choice. After that, our piña coladas are really good," he said.

"Okay. I'll take the peach mojito since that's your first choice."

The waiter smiled. "I'll tell you what; how about the mojitos are on the house and you give me your phone number."

Nikki and I laughed. *She did it again!* I thought. Nikki was great at getting us discounts everywhere we went. I was inspired by it. As I watched them exchange phone numbers, I started to wonder if I should tell her about my diagnosis. I really wanted to. That was one of the main reasons I wanted to grab a drink with her, but I didn't want to ruin our good time.

Look at Nikki ... For one thing, Nikki is not dark like you, and for another, she is beautiful and confident. Taneshia, you're so-so looking, but you will never have the confidence she has. Just do you. Get good grades, get your license, and continue to heal the world. Don't you know this is what God wants you to do? Everybody can't be Beyoncé and Rihanna. Just be Plain Jane Taneshia. What's with all this changing all of a sudden?

I didn't care what my internal thoughts were telling me. I was ready for a transformation. Therapy had sparked a change in me. I remembered when I used to put on makeup, try new hairstyles, new clothes, and be more confident. I wanted to get back to that girl. I was done being the brokenhearted girl. If I were to be honest with myself, Shawn was not on my level nor was he the kind of man I deserved. I wanted a man who pursued career goals. I needed a man who was emotionally intelligent and knew I was loving, kind, and would support him to the fullest but also understood that I struggled with anxiety, and I worried often, but I just needed an encouraging word to get on my feet.

I heard Nikki calling my name, and I saw two mojitos in front of us.

"Taneshia, Taneshia, you tired, girl? What's up? Look what we got. For free! Holla!"

Nikki and I slapped hands.

"I want to toast to great friendship and sisterhood," Nikki said.

I smiled, glanced at my drink and paused. I raised my glass. "I want to toast to a new life of loving me, accepting my flaws, and gaining insight on who I am."

Nikki smiled and took a sip. "Yes, child! That's what I'm talking about. Beautiful Taneshia unfolding before my eyes. Thank you, God! I will drink to that, sweetie!"

We both laughed.

"Nikki, I have so much to tell you, I don't know where to start. I'm just going to dive in."

"Okay, wait. Let me sip my drink first." She took a long sip of her mojito and looked at me eagerly. "Okay, girl, spill the tea!" Nikki said.

"I have been going to therapy and support groups for about

a month now, and I have been diagnosed with depression and anxiety."

I watched Nikki's entire face drop. Her eyes suddenly grew big. She grabbed my hand from across the table. "Taneshia, I am so proud of you! Yes, Queen! I am so happy you're finally seeing your light. I've been worried about you. We all struggle, but you've been coming to class late, wearing t-shirts and sweats all the time. I didn't know what was going on, but I saw the signs of depression. That's why I told Ron, Lisa, Angela, and T that we needed to check in on you and make sure you're doing okay. You're an awesome social worker. You're a natural at helping people. I'm so happy to hear you're taking care of *you*!"

"Thank you. It's a scary place to be in. I often worry about how people will respond to me putting myself first, but that's still me worrying about other people and not me."

"I remember you telling me about a group you were starting at your church. Are you facilitating?" Nikki asked.

"Originally, that was the plan, but I had to back out once I discovered I needed support."

"Yaassssss! Putting you first! I say that deserves another toast!"

We raised our glasses and sipped. The server dropped off our food, and we both were eager to eat. I reflected on my progress. When struggling with codependency, others' needs and wants were more important. Knowing what I needed was new to me. It felt surreal. I liked learning about what I needed. I liked learning about my emotions. I was teaching myself how to feel. I was learning about the feelings I had and what they meant to me.

Therapy was giving me a voice. It was becoming a place I

could go to understand my reactions, responses, and my past. I was learning how to put myself first. It may be cliché, but putting myself first was easier said than done when struggling with codependency. My existence was embedded into other people's emotions. I changed my plans constantly based on others' needs. If my cousin or family members needed money, I changed plans I had for myself. When my clients needed to change their appointments, I would stay at work for hours to meet them later, even if I was tired and not getting paid overtime. I had learned to assess people quickly and respond to their emotions. It was a great skill to have, but codependent people struggle to provide themselves with the same level of care, which creates the inability to know how to be in tune and provide for themselves.

Nikki and I stayed at the restaurant for a few hours laughing, joking, and reflecting on life. It was the first time in a long time I had gone out with a friend and had fun, and I was so happy I had chosen Nikki.

I drove home feeling accomplished. Life was really turning around for me. I was going out with friends, putting on some of my favorite outfits, and I wasn't allowing my negative thoughts to dictate choices I made anymore.

When I pulled up to my carport, I thought of the things I had to do for the following week. "Aww man, I still need to do my homework for Dr. Jones," I said aloud.

I walked into my apartment, said goodnight to my mom, and started looking through old photos of myself as a child. I was a cute little thing. Every picture showed me smiling happily and wearing a designer outfit with matching barrettes my mom had bought. She took good care of me. In the background were my toys, room, and stuffed animals. We didn't have much, but I always had what I needed and most of what I wanted. My dad had missed the first five years of my life. I was told I saw my father early on, but the first memory I had was when I was six years old. Dr. Jones said the picture I chose to reflect on should be of myself at the age I was when I first remembered feeling sad. I found a picture of myself when I was six. I was in the first grade. I went to a Catholic school, so I had on a red sweater and plaid dress. My smile was big with missing teeth, and I had red knockers and barrettes in my hair.

As I looked at the picture, I connected with the image of myself as a child. Dr. Jones was correct. Memories of myself at that age flooded my head. I burned a candle and got on my knees in prayer position. I looked at the image for several minutes.

I started to cry as I remembered how I felt back then. After a few tears fell, I decided to talk and just let my thoughts flow.

"Little Taneshia, I am so sorry for what happened to you. I know you often felt unloved and unwanted. The only friend you had was Diane. I want you to know that, even though it didn't feel like it sometimes, both of your parents loved you very much. In many ways, they gave you what they didn't get themselves. Because of you, I am here. We are here. I promise to love you, be a voice for you, and protect you. Trust me and know that I have to change the ways we use to cope. Food was your comfort, but it can't be mine. We are sick now. We have diabetes, and it's not under control. You didn't speak up for yourself. You allowed people to use and manipulate you, but I can't do that anymore. I have to be assertive and tell people how I feel. We can't take care of other people anymore and hope they don't abandon us or get upset. We have to take care of ourselves and trust that God will send people in our life who will love us the way we deserve."

I was crying so much I had to pause and grab some tissues.

"Taneshia, I love you, and I thank you for everything you went through so we can have this moment."

I got up from my knees and lay on my bed, staring at the candle burning on my nightstand. Memories flashed into my mind, everything that had happened between the ages of six to the present. I reflected on missing my dad growing up, wondering why he hadn't sacrificed for me and moved back to California when he found out I was born. I thought about Shawn. How could I have been so stupid to think he really cared about me? I didn't put all the blame on Shawn. I was using him as a way to escape my life. I questioned if I really wanted to be with him or felt like I had no other options because of my low self-esteem.

Therapy was bringing out a lot for me. It had me self-reflecting on so many areas of my life. I saw myself transforming into someone I didn't know. Thinking about me was a skill I knew nothing about, but I was learning how. I knew God had the power to bring me through.

I stood and took all my clothes off. I found a nightgown in my closet and lay on my bed. "Dear God, whatever happens in my life, I want You to know I am ready. I am ready to live the life You desire for me. I am still figuring out how I got here, but one thing I do know is that I don't want to stay here. I love You. Amen."

I gazed out the window, amazed that I was going to sleep without crying for the second time.

CHAPTER 7

WHAT IS ANXIETY AND HOW DID I GET IT?

It was time to make some action steps toward my new life. I had been searching for a new job for a while, and one finally came through. I was beyond happy to give my notice to David. I got to work early that Monday with my resignation letter in hand. I knew I could count on David to already be there in *my* office instead of his own. He normally started the week by checking on my attendance and me.

"Well, well, well ... Good morning, Taneshia." David stood when he saw me walk into the office.

"Good morning. How was your weekend?" I said.

"The weekend was okay, but this morning is great. My number-one employee is on time to work! Hey, I can go home now." He laughed.

"Number one?" I asked, confused.

"Yeah, Taneshia, you're a great employee. I know that, and

your colleagues know that. I want to work with you about your attendance, and we need to work as a team to learn not to share our department issues with others."

"I'm confused by all of this. What are you talking about? Because at the meeting, you yelled and looked directly at me. All I did was go to the bathroom, so I was confused. Now, you're saying I'm your number-one employee?"

My thoughts flooded my mind, and my body grew stiff. I felt tears trying to form in my eyes, but I held them back.

Taneshia, calm down, okay? Just wait. Things seem to be headed in the right direction. Maybe ask him for a raise instead of leaving. This new job may be even worse. You have flexibility here. Where else can you take two-hour lunches and get your hair done during the day? Girl, be smart. Be cool.

I decided not to listen to my thoughts. I was leaving and that was that.

"Taneshia, uh ... I don't know what to say. I have never had an issue with you past your attendance. I mean, I tell you that all the time. You do a great job," David said.

"Are you serious? You never tell me what a great job I do. You hire new staff and make them supervisor over me, even though I have more experience. All you ever do is complain about my attendance, which, in my opinion, isn't bad at all. Do you know how many days I work late, how many times I have seen clients late just to provide good service?" I dropped my bag and placed the envelope with my resignation inside on the desk.

"Taneshia, I'm glad we're having this conversation because you need to know I have never felt like you were a bad employee. I was told by another supervisor that some of the staff were sharing things we talk about in our meetings, but that person was not you," he said, looking frantic and desperate for me to understand him.

"I see. Well, you know what; it's all good now." I picked up the envelope and handed it to him. "David, I am leaving. My new position starts in three weeks. I figured I would give you an extra week's notice to ensure you can hire someone, and I can train them. I want our clients to get the best service possible regardless of how I feel." I was feeling confident with a smile I didn't want to remove. "I have been suffering at this job for years now. I've been unhappy here. You've transferred me from one office to the next with no notice. You talk to me any way you desire, and often, I feel disrespected by you on many levels. Your mannerisms with me have been inappropriate and street like. Last week, you stepped in front of my face like you were going to fight me and removed your glasses. What was that? But it's all good. I forgive you."

David sat and leaned on the desk. "Taneshia, I can't believe this. Wow! You're leaving? I apologize for anything I may have done, but your view of things is wrong. I always knew you were a great employee."

"Thank you for saying that, but the way I feel about a situation is never wrong. Perhaps you didn't mean to come off like you did, but at the end of the day, I did not feel safe, and I can no longer stay in this work environment."

"Okay, I understand. Well, please send an email to the staff saying that you're leaving, and I will take your resignation letter to HR. I am really sorry to see you go."

And that was it. David walked out of the office with his head down. I closed the door behind him and started to cry. "Thank you, Jesus. Thank you, Jesus. I got you, Little Taneshia. We getting the hell out of this toxic environment. He is a narcissist to the tenth power! Trying to make me feel crazy as if none of those things happened. Thank you, Jesus! I am free!"

At six p.m., I walked out the door carrying some of my belongings. Why not get a head start on cleaning out my desk?

I hopped into my car and drove off, smiling while playing one of my favorite CDs, Mary J. Blige's *My Life* album. As I drove on the freeway, singing the melody and snapping my fingers, I felt proud of myself for making a move for me. I had been dying emotionally and mentally for the last three years at that job, but it wasn't just the job; it was my entire life. Changing jobs was the kick start I needed to put me first.

As I got closer to my apartment, I started feeling sick. I was having a hard time breathing, and my left hand was numb. I didn't know what to do. I pulled over and prayed.

"Lord what is happening?" I looked in my rearview mirror and saw there were hardly any cars on the road. I didn't know if I should call 9-1-1 or try to flag a car down. I thought to call my mom but knew she would only be worried, and her feelings would increase my anxiety. I had that feeling again—alone, having no one. As tears flowed from my eyes, I said another prayer. "Dear God, I don't know what's happening. I'm scared. I don't have anyone but You. Please guide me to the hospital, and please don't let anything be wrong."

I got back onto the freeway and started off to the closest hospital about eight miles away. Those miles felt so far. I turned my CD player off. Nothing but pure silence accompanied me in the car. As I cried, I could hear my heart beating faster.

"What is this?" I asked aloud. "Lord, if I'm dying, please forgive me of my sins. I don't know what I did, but I'm sorry." The pain in my chest grew stronger, and I began to sweat. My hands were numb. I thought I was having a heart attack. I prayed to make it to the hospital before dying inside my car.

I pulled up to the hospital and found a parking space. I was used to being sick, so I already had my I.D. and medical insurance card in my hand. I knew the protocol and wanted to be seen quickly.

"Hello, my name is Taneshia Johnson. I'm having chest pains and want to be seen by a doctor." I felt my heart pumping increasingly faster. I was calm while talking to the nurse. I concluded that if I was dying, at least I was in the hospital, so there was no need to work myself up. The nurse looked into my eyes and saw the emerging tears.

"Are you okay, sweetie?" she asked as she handed me some tissue.

"No. I drove myself here, and I can't feel my left hand," I said through my tears. I don't know how I learned to cry in silence. Most of my life, I assumed no one cared about my tears and how I felt, so I didn't see a need to ask people for support or nurturing. It felt good for someone to acknowledge that I was sad.

"Okay, sweetie. Try not to worry. You're in the right place. Have a seat, and a nurse will call you shortly." She pointed to the red chairs on the opposite side of the room.

I walked over and took a seat.

What have you done this time? You haven't been taking care of yourself the way you're supposed to. You know they're going to blame this on your high blood sugar numbers, right? You can't do anything right. If you took your insulin and stopped eating, you wouldn't have this problem. You thought a new job would make you feel better? Yeah, right. Look around. Does this look familiar?

You are in the hospital alone! *I keep telling you, you don't have anyone. I wish you would listen to me.*

I sat in silence, looking at the floor, and cried. The tears ran down my chin and onto my clothes. It seemed like after every step I made toward happiness, I was knocked five steps back. My thoughts were right. This scene was familiar. Physically, I was thirty, but emotionally, I was sixteen. I had turned into that sixteen-year-old girl in the hospital being treated by strange people I didn't know. I allowed my tears to follow. I talked to God. He was all I had. "Dear God, I am so scared. Please let everything be okay. I haven't been taking care of my health, but please give me a chance to show You I can." I began getting worked up, and my heart started pounding in my chest. I went to the bathroom so I could finish my prayer.

"I'm going to the restroom for a minute," I told the nurse.

I saw sympathy in her eyes. "Okay, honey. Try not to work yourself up. You made it here, and it's going to be okay."

I managed to put a smile on my face despite the tears in my eyes. "Okay."

I walked to the bathroom and immediately began crying louder. "Ugh! I am so tired. I'm so tired!" I screamed. The tears and screams spilled out of me.

I heard my phone ring. It was my mom.

"Hello?" I answered, wiping my eyes and trying not to sound like I had just been crying my eyes out.

"Where are you? Are you okay?" my mom asked.

"No. I'm at the emergency room. I can't feel my left hand or arm, and my heart is beating fast."

"You're having palpitations. What happened? Did your supervisor say something to you again?" She sounded angry.

"No, no. I don't know what happened. I was happy when I left the job, and all of a sudden, it came on."

"Okay, I'm coming down there," she said.

"No, it's okay. Hopefully, I'll be out of here soon." I didn't want my mom to come and get upset.

"Are you sure?"

"Yes. It's okay. I can hear someone calling my name. I'll call you back, Mama."

"Okay, Taneshia. Tell them *all* your symptoms, and make sure they know you're diabetic. Call me with updates." Ever since my mom found out I was diabetic, she made it a mission to teach me how to state exactly how I felt and what symptoms I had to doctors.

"Yes, ma'am," I said and hung up.

I walked out of the stall and saw a nurse standing there. She had on blue and white scrubs, and her hair was in a ponytail. "Hi. I'm Betty. I'll be helping you today. Let's get your vitals."

"Okay."

As we walked to the blood pressure machine and scale, I started having thoughts. But they were different. It felt real, like a voice in my head torturing me.

Here we go again, Taneshia. You know these vitals are gonna come out all messed up. Now, you have high blood pressure and diabetes. You can barely breathe. You might as well get comfortable. You know you're gonna be admitted. You just got this new job! I don't know how you do it, but you find a way to mess up everything for yourself.

As the nurse prepared the blood pressure monitor, she glanced at me and smiled, but she instantly frowned when she saw my face. "Oh no, honey, what's wrong? Don't be worried, okay? You're young. I'm sure your blood pressure is fine. This is just procedure." She handed me some tissue.

I wanted to tell someone about my thoughts. She'd seen the tears, but if she knew what my thoughts were telling me, she would know why I was crying. I didn't know what my thoughts meant. I was ashamed to tell people that I felt like I was going crazy, and even if I did, how would I explain it? Dr. Jones said they were called intrusive thoughts and it was common with anxiety. Because I spent so much of my life believing I was worthless and couldn't do anything right, I was also making life decisions based on those beliefs. Anxiety had taken over my mind and, now, it appeared, my body. I was still trying to figure out what it meant for me. I wasn't ready to share it with someone else. It felt too complicated, so I decided to cry in silence.

"Hold your arm out for me, honey," she said.

As I extended my left arm, I saw that my sweater and arm were wet from my tears. "Oh no, sweetie, it's okay. Let's wipe off your arm. How could someone with such a beautiful smile like yours cry? It's okay, honey. Don't worry." She wiped my arm off and placed the blood pressure cuff on.

As the cuff grew tighter on my arm, I tensed up. I heard the voice again.

No need to tense up now. It's going to be high. You should've gone out on medical leave. Why did you sacrifice your time and health for this job? Still trying to be perfect, Taneshia. Look where you are now! Taking care of everybody else got you back in the hospital. Wake up! You're not super social worker, super friend, super daughter, or even super church member. You are human! You're about to get the break you've been praying for—another four days in the hospital.

As the nurse removed the cuff from my arm, I cried while glancing at the machine.

"Look, sweetie! You're fine! One twenty-one over seventy-two. That's very good, especially considering your fast heart rate. I told you everything would be fine. Let's get your weight next."

"Do we have to?" I asked softly.

"Yes, unfortunately, we do. Don't worry. It's okay."

I looked at her in amazement. How could she be so positive? She didn't know me or my life. Yet every time she'd said it would be okay, so far, it was. I wondered if I should start telling myself things would be okay.

"Sweetie, get on the scale for me, okay?"

As I boarded the scale, I told myself it would be okay. It would be less than I thought.

"Good news! You've lost five pounds from last time!"

"Really?" I said.

"Is that a smile I see on your face? Finally, girl! Yeah, don't worry. Have you been anxious about anything?" she asked while writing down my weight and blood pressure number on a board.

"Yes. I've been going through a lot of changes for a little over a month."

She's so sweet, I thought. She gave me a hug and told me to have a seat in the waiting room.

I sat there quietly, thinking about what just happened. Every time the nurse said things would be okay, they were. *Where did she learn that? And how was she so sure?* It was like she'd had a premonition. It reminded me of when I was younger and the faith and trust I had in God. I loved God and knew He could work miracles for me, but I felt like I had done something to keep His love away from me. Hearing her say those positive affirmations gave me hope.

"Hi, honey. I'm the EKG technician. I need you to lie down so I can check your heart."

Who the hell is this? And why are they checking my heart? "Where is the doctor?" I asked.

"The doctor will be in shortly, but we need to do this EKG because you stated that you're having chest pains. You still are, correct?"

"Yeah, but..." I gasped, trying to find a way to tell her I didn't want to take the test.

"Okay, lie back."

It looked like this was happening whether I wanted it to or not, so I lay back. She placed what looked like stickers on my stomach and chest. Each one was attached to a tube.

Oh, my goodness! What is this? This is just like before. Look at you! You're connected to all these tubes just like last time. Oh, my God! You should have told your mother to come. She gets these done all the time. She could have instructed you. Now you're alone. These sticky things are cold, too. Say something to the nurse, fool! We don't need all this!

"Everything is going to be fine," I said aloud.

The technician chuckled. "That's right, sweetie! Your test results came out fine. No abnormalities. You must have had a panic attack. Do you have them often?"

"No, I never had one," I said, but then I thought about it. When Shawn had left me in Las Vegas, I had a pain in my chest. I was in such shock that I ignored it. While waiting for my client at the cupcake shop, I had chest pains. It had come again when my supervisor yelled at me in front of everyone. Maybe they were panic attacks and I didn't realize it. "Actually, I have before," I confessed. "I guess I didn't realize what they were."

"Hmm, okay. Yes, I think that's what it was. Have you been going through a lot of stress?" she asked, holding my arm.

I looked at her, how she was holding my arm. She seemed like a safe person to share with, but I didn't want to tell anyone about the thoughts. "I struggle with depression and anxiety," I said, holding my head down. Although I had accepted the diagnosis, it was still hard to share with people.

"We all struggle with something. Don't beat yourself up over it."

That comment seemed to roll off everyone's tongues so easily. I wished I could stop beating myself up, but that's who I was. Sometimes I felt like it wasn't even me. It was the voice I couldn't get out of my head that told me negative things about myself all the time. The first nurse, who reassured me everything would be fine, made an impression on me. I decided I would try saying those positive things to myself next time my inner thoughts started to take over.

The doctor and the first nurse, Betty, came in. "Hi, Taneshia. How are you feeling?" He smiled.

"I'm okay. I'm learning I may have had a panic attack."

"Yes, your EKG was great, heart images great, blood pressure good, and you've lost five pounds since the last time you saw your primary care doctor. The nurse stated that you've been under a lot of stress. I saw that you spoke with a mental health clinician. Do you struggle with anxiety, Taneshia?"

"Yes, I was recently diagnosed with general anxiety by my therapist."

"Are you still meeting with that therapist?" He wrote as he asked me questions.

"Yes, I am."

"I'm going to prescribe some medication that can help you with your panic attacks. I recommend you continue therapy and find ways to manage your anxiety and speak with your primary care doctor," he said.

"Okay. Thank you so much."

The nurse gave me the release papers to sign with instructions for the medication and told me to follow up with my doctor. I took the papers and put on my clothes. I had forgotten I was connected to the EKG machine. As I removed each sticker from my body, I was reminded of being connected to machines when I was sixteen.

"I don't want to be this person anymore," I said aloud to myself. "I need to really start taking care of myself."

It took me almost five minutes to get all the stickers off my body, but I finally removed them and put my clothes and shoes on. I checked my hair and face in the mirror and left the room.

As I got into my car, my brain started working on how I could take care of myself. It would involve more than just eating right and exercise. I was overweight and diabetic, but I felt my eating habits were triggered by my daily experiences. I ate because I was exhausted from constantly helping people around me and being there for everyone all the time. I didn't exercise because, by the time I got home, I was tired and had no energy for myself. The problem was my lack of ability to control other people, but what did that mean?

I had so many random thoughts that I got home before I realized it.

"What happened? You okay?" my mom asked as she walked toward the door. I could tell she was worried.

"I'm okay. They said I had a panic attack," I said.

She looked at me, confused. "Panic attack? You don't have those. How do they know?"

"They hooked me up to the EKG and ran images on my heart, and everything was fine, so they said it must have been a panic attack." I shrugged. I was getting nervous again just telling her.

"Okay, well it's late. I'm going to bed. Get some rest. I'm glad you feel better." She gave me a kiss and went to bed.

I went to my room, still trying to figure out what was happening. I knew codependency had something to do with this, but I didn't know how to control it. I decided I should tell Dr. Jones about it and return to the support group at my church and see if anyone had insight. I was determined to find a way to finally end my inner thoughts and find joy again.

I woke up the next day and called out sick from work, leaving a message for David explaining what happened the previous night. Part of me was hoping he felt bad for what he had done, but I decided not to focus on being the victim but focus on how I could better my life for myself. I called Dr. Jones to see if she had an opening that day instead of Wednesday. I wanted to see her while the memory of being hospitalized was fresh.

She agreed to see me at two p.m.

I glanced at the clock and saw that it was nine a.m. I decided to take a nap and set my alarm for noon. Learning to take care of myself was new, but I felt like I was getting the hang of it.

Noon came, and it was time to get ready. I glanced inside my closet and found some cute dark jeans, tank top, and sandals. As I dressed, I looked at myself in the mirror. "Wow! You are beautiful." I smiled in amazement. I was getting used to seeing myself in real clothes again.

I drove to Dr. Jones's office and found a parking spot in the front. I walked up to her door and rang the doorbell.

"Good afternoon, Taneshia," she said with a smile.

"Hi, Doctor. How are you?"

"I'm well. How are you?"

"Not that good," I said, hopping onto the recliner and dropping my purse on the floor.

"Okay, let's talk about it. I hope the exercise went okay."

"The exercise was amazing! Some parts were difficult. I didn't realize how much I had been through at such a young age. The memories flooded my mind."

"Mmm. Yes, yes. That is common. How were your thoughts? Did they disrupt the process?"

"No," I said with a big smile. "I was shocked, Dr. Jones!"

She chuckled. "Great, Taneshia. This is great news. Share with me some things you said to Little Taneshia."

"I told her I appreciate and thank her for all she did to cope with life for us during that time, but things are different now. I told her I would love her and stand up for her, and she no longer had to be codependent and cope with food."

Dr. Jones reclined in her seat. "Wow, Taneshia. I think I may need some tissue this session. I am amazed and so happy to see how you are pressing forward. Awesome!"

"Aw, thank you. I owe it all to you. And, of course, God. I feel God sent you to me. I had been trying to figure out my next steps for a while. Turning thirty seemed to send me to an emotional place I didn't know how to deal with. Until I came to see you, I didn't know what I was feeling. Honestly, I didn't know how to feel. I thought I was just going through life being subjected to what everyone else needed. I didn't think about my feelings."

"I know. Our first few sessions, you didn't even know what a feeling was. I could tell you weren't used to people asking you how you felt. Many people aren't. As you complete your graduate program, you will learn techniques to use on your clients, but, honestly, there are healthy communication skills we should be using all the time." Dr. Jones crossed her legs and put her notebook down. I liked the fact that Dr. Jones was getting comfortable around me.

"We only have a few sessions left, huh?" I said with a grudge.

"Yes, we have about two left, but don't worry. I have a sliding scale option for you. Let's not focus on that yet. Taneshia, when you think too much about the future, it ignites your anxiety, which, in turn, creates the thoughts, crying, and physical responses like your panic attacks and shaking hands. Remember, I want you to work on being present and saying positive affirmations about yourself and your experiences. I appreciate your concern, but we have time to work that out. Let's talk about whatever you were going to share when you came into session today." Dr. Jones picked her notebook back up and started writing.

"Okay, well, I gave my notice to my supervisor this week, and in the process, I experienced a panic attack. I discovered I have them often. The ER doctor prescribed some meds that I have decided not to take. However, I do feel that therapy and going back to my support group at church will help me."

"Mm hm. I see. I believe continuing to meet and going to

the support group will help. Taneshia, how do you feel about going to the support group every week and maybe even going to a CODA group."

"CODA? What is that?"

"Codependent Anonymous."

"Uh, there's so much happening for me right now. I'm starting a new job, I'm still in school, and seeing you and going to my church group is already a lot for me."

"I see. Well, I understand, but know that there are groups specifically for codependents that are open to you." She looked at the clock. "I am so sorry, but we've run out of time. Your homework for this week is to go to your support group and share with them what you've been experiencing."

"What? You mean share what I've been talking about with you?" I was confused. The things I had discovered about myself while working with her I considered private. Plus, I didn't want everyone to know I was crazy. I mean, yes, it was a support group, but it was also my church family, people I had to see every Sunday.

"You can share anything you want. It doesn't have to be things we talk about, but I do want you to be more vulnerable in the group than you usually are. I brought up CODA groups because that would give you a space where no one knows you, and you can speak freely. You want to end the thoughts or voices, right?"

"Yes, I really do."

"Then this is the first step. Being honest in the program. This group of people know you as Social Worker Taneshia, Helpful Taneshia, who listens to all their problems. I don't want you to show up as that person. I want you to show up as that little girl like you do here in session. Be honest about your recovery and reach out for support. Can you do that?"

"Yes, yes, I can." I grabbed my purse, and Dr. Jones and I hugged and shook hands.

"I'll see you next week. And remember to show up as Little Taneshia. Give her a voice."

I smiled and replied, "Okay."

Dr. Jones was asking for a lot, but she was right. I needed to be vulnerable and reach out for support. I didn't want to find a CODA group. I wanted to be more consistent with my church group because I knew they cared, and I felt comfortable.

CHAPTER 8

A POWER GREATER THAN ME CAN HEAL ME

I took off the rest of the week from work. I knew I was leaving my job soon and I had clients to see, but I didn't worry about them. It was about me and my health.

Friday approached quickly, and that morning, I woke up in a daze. *Did this week really happen, or did I imagine it?* I hoped I was having a bad dream and I wouldn't feel hopeless about my life again. I had just started feeling like I was in control. I was starting a great job in a couple of weeks, and things were looking up for me. I didn't want to face the reality that my life was still unmanageable.

In the curriculum we used at the support group, I discovered that thinking I was in control was part of my denial. I was never in control. The people I was taking care of were controlling me. Anytime anyone needed anything, I was there: family, friends, coworkers, even strangers. It was like I had a gravitational pull to other people's needs that I couldn't turn off. I had to face the reality that living like that wasn't working for me.

Between working full-time and school on Saturday, I had no life. I was struggling to spend time with friends and family, so going to a support group every Friday didn't feel like it would fit into my schedule. However, after speaking with Dr. Jones, I realized it was necessary to be there and finally put my needs first.

I parked my car outside of the church and sat there for a few minutes. I hadn't been to the group in a few weeks and was nervous about telling people the many things I had discovered about myself including my struggle with codependency. But other people pulled their cars up behind mine, and I was stuck.

"Is that you, Taneshia? Hey, girl! Good to see you, friend. It's about time you came back!" my friend Janice said, laughing.

I chuckled and gave her a hug. I loved to have Janice in my presence and hated when she left because her conversation was genuine, and her love was real. I was happy to see that she made it that night. Her warm smile and hug made me feel more confident as I walked into the building.

"Look who I found, everybody!" Janice yelled as we walked into the church.

"Taneshia!" everyone yelled with big smiles and open arms.

I felt so loved. Suddenly, someone grabbed me from behind. I turned to the side and saw it was Roland. "How you doing, there, Taneshia? Amen, sister. Praise God! I have been praying for you, Amen. So glad to see you back."

"Thank you. I've missed you, too."

Roland was a true man of God's Word and a realist. He found it important that people be honest about what they were going through, and he practiced honesty and transparency with his feelings during his own recovery.

"I have been going to therapy every week. Now that I know I'm codependent and have accepted it, I pray I don't relapse to old ways of people pleasing. This is a new way of living for me, and it feels so hard."

"Now, Taneshia, we have to back track what you just said. Don't be ashamed to relapse. Relapse is a part of recovery. Let's think about it. What is a relapse? A relapse is when we decide to do our own thing and forget about what God has for us. We go into our old ways, instead of talking to God and working on the program. Therefore, if we relapse, there's no need to fear because we can always return to God, sister."

I started to cry, and he embraced me with a hug. "Yes, yes, Amen. I was in denial about the help I really need from God to learn a different way of life, but I'm glad I see clearly now," I admitted, stuttering over my tears as I wiped my eyes.

"It's all right, sister," Roland said while holding my hand. "Praise God that you're here tonight. Tell the group all about your feelings when it's time for you to share."

Sharing time in our group was when we shared our experiences in recovery without interruption, whether good or bad.

The group was starting. I ran to the kitchen. I wasn't going to be able to sit amongst everyone and express the truth without some food in my stomach. I grabbed grapes, broccoli, and chips and salsa and sat next to Janice. I looked at my plate and smiled, happy that I was making healthier food choices. I was healing.

"Hi, everyone. Thank you for coming to another night of Recovery! You could have been anywhere else, but you came here. Give yourself a round of applause," Geneva said.

We read the twelve steps out loud before each group. There were seven of us, and we went around the table. My turn came to read.

I read the sixth step. My voice was shaky at first. "Step six: You are entirely ready to have God remove all these defects of character. 'Humble yourself before the Lord, and He will lift you up' (James 4:10 NIV)." I finally understood what that verse meant. Change was a process, and it wouldn't happen unless I was ready. The events that had occurred showed me that my life was unmanageable, and I *needed* God's help. I had a clear understanding of my experiences and the outcomes. The panic attacks, intrusive thoughts, and negative self-image all came from my lack of faith and trust in God. I didn't believe that God had the power to make my situation better if I allowed Him to. I was afraid to fully let Him take over my life because I didn't have control over the outcome. However, I never had control over the outcome. I only thought I did.

I sat there in a daze for a while, shocked that I was back in this space, ready to share my feelings and emotions about who I was and what I was experiencing. I decided I was ready to tell the group what I had been going through. I didn't know how to do it, so I let my thoughts pour out of my mouth. "Hi, my name is Taneshia, and I'm a recovering codependent who struggles with overeating, anxiety, and depression."

"Hi, Taneshia," everyone said.

"I haven't been here in a few weeks. I want to start by thanking everyone who texted and called me, and thank you all for the warm welcome. It really made me feel good." I could feel my face getting warm and tears welling in my eyes. A group member gave me some tissue, and I continued. "It's been a hard road. School has been so stressful. I had to change jobs, and everything has been a mess. I thought I would be happy once I turned in my resignation letter, but I'm still not." I wiped my eyes and blew my nose. "So I decided to come back home. Come back to you all. I realized, just now, while reading the steps, that I'm still not giving God power over things in my life. I'm taking on other people's problems in addition to my own, thinking I can help everyone. I can't even solve my own problems without God; I don't know why I feel I can solve anyone else's." I shook my head, confused about why I had those thoughts in the first place.

"I am so tired, so tired. I just want to be happy. I don't want to worry about anyone or anything anymore. I just want to be Taneshia and focus on my own life. The sad part is people don't even realize the stress they put on me because I put it on myself and never complain about it. I take it upon myself to help everybody. I guess I'm really tired of me."

Roland was next to me. He put his hand on my shoulder. "Sister Taneshia, I know we're not supposed to interrupt people," he started while looking at Geneva.

Geneva gave him the evil eye because he knew that interrupting people during open share was against the rules, but she allowed him to speak.

"First and foremost, Taneshia, stop beating yourself up. You know how many people there are in your same condition who need to be at this church with us right now? Praise God, sister, that you realized that your life has become unmanageable. What does the Bible tell us, you all? In Proverbs, it says, 'Trust in the Lord with all your heart, and He will direct your path.' It doesn't say trust in Taneshia, Roland, Janice, Geneva, or any of us at this table. It says trust in the *Lord*. We need God to help us. God has the healing power, sister. We don't. That's why you're tired, burned out, walking around looking like you need to be in the mental hospital. People can see you're broken, Taneshia. You're not hiding it as well as you think you are. Okay, I'm gonna be quiet because I know I went over my time and broke the rules, but I had to say that, y'all. Amen. Continue on, sister."

Geneva looked upset, like she was about to chastise Roland. I raised my hand. "It's all right, Auntie Geneva. It's true. I have been moving through this life, thinking I'm God, and I have the power to help everyone. I have been using everyone else as a distraction because I didn't believe I could be whole. I thought my life was so broken that there was no way it could be fixed. I *do* beat myself up *a lot*. Believe it or not, I have thoughts in my head daily, telling me I'm crazy." I laughed, and the whole group laughed, too.

Geneva blurted, "We all struggle with something, Taneshia. You're not alone here. We are honest with ourselves and each other. That's why we're healing."

I smiled and looked around the room. It was true. I wasn't the only person who was codependent or had negative thoughts. I thought about past stories I had heard from some of them that were like mine.

"Amen," Janice said. "We're all here only by God's grace, Taneshia. You are never alone. I stand with you. We all do. We all know what it's like to feel so beat down you can't even get up, to wonder how things are going to happen in your life because it feels like every door is closed. That's when we need God the most."

Roland got excited and stood. "Amen! Say that, Janice! Now,

Taneshia just opened up the floodgates. Amen! I have thoughts all the time! Sometimes, I talk back to them!"

We all laughed and hugged each other.

As I embraced and connected with my fellow brothers and sisters in Christ, I noticed I didn't have any negative thoughts. I hadn't had any for a few days, ever since I'd left the hospital. It was as if having a panic attack and seeing myself chained to all those tubes awakened something inside me. It was a reminder that I didn't want to live my life like that anymore—alone, caregiving, being a people pleaser, and, most importantly, living a life of codependency. I felt safe in the group. I hadn't felt safe anywhere for a long time.

We completed the lesson for the night, and I drove home. No negative thoughts and no tears. Just me, God, and the peace I had inside knowing that life from here on out was going to get a whole lot better.

CHAPTER 9

MINDFULNESS BROUGHT ME JOY

On Saturday morning, I got up early. I wanted to do some research on how people have overcome codependency before I went to school. I had become somewhat obsessed with codependency and began watching self-help videos to determine how to start breaking the chains of people pleasing. I was progressing well in therapy and the support group at my church. I wanted to find ways to work on myself when I was on my own.

Dr. Jones had given me a lot to think about with our past sessions. I noticed every session seemed to spark a desire to discover more about myself, so I didn't fight it. I came across a famous psychologist named Abraham Maslow. He created a pyramid for a hierarchy of needs. He determined that if a person hasn't met basic needs in their life such as food, water, and shelter, it would be difficult for them to focus on any other area of their life. He concluded that for someone to reach their full potential in life and be comfortable with who they are and know where they're going, certain areas must be covered.

I looked at the graph and tried to determine where I was. The first level was psychological needs: food, water, and shelter. I was good there. Second was safety needs: security and safety. That area in my life was good as well. Third: belongingness and feelings of being loved. That area definitely needed work. Others loved me, but I didn't love myself. Fourth area: feelings of accomplishments and prestige. I felt like I had too much of that already. Last: self-actualization and achieving one's full potential, including creative activities. I felt I was stuck on the third tier. My need to be loved was preventing me from moving up the tier to self-actualization. I had often read self-help articles I did not like, but this one really bothered me. How in the world would I get there? I sat there for a while, staring at the form and concluded that Abraham Maslow's pyramid was not the right graph to use when it came to finding my own joy and learning how to live a life recovering from codependency.

I decided to create my own. In my process of recovery, a few things had become clear to me. First, to go through this process of change, I wasn't going to be able to expect results overnight. Secondly, I would need to stay close to God and trust in Him and the healing process, not in me.

The first step toward learning to be my own light and change was self-awareness. My unhappiness forced me to look at my life for what it was, not what I imagined it to be. My reality was that I did what others wanted me to do out of fear that they wouldn't love me if I didn't. The next step was acceptance. I had to accept that life as it was currently was not working for me.

In the process of keeping everyone else happy, I was miserable and didn't feel loved, even though feeling loved was the reason I aimed to please others. The next step I took was an obligation to myself to change. I was responsible for my own happiness. I knew what was wrong and now owed it to myself to get the help and support I needed.

Next up was forgiveness. I had to forgive myself for the years of people pleasing, the time I'd spent fulfilling others' dreams instead of focusing on my own. I had to forgive other people who had hurt me. This part seemed hard, but I was learning to accept that people do the best they know how to do, and I couldn't expect anything else. I forgave myself for my negative thoughts and believing what they told me about who I was. I had forgotten that I was a child of God, worthy of love and anything I desired. I didn't need others to love me, I could love me and do a better job. Like Dr. Jones had told me, my inner child, Little Taneshia, dealt with a lot. She went through all kinds of hoops trying to get people to love her. I owed it to myself to shower myself with love. Self-love was what I really needed all along.

After writing all the steps, I looked at the graph. As I reflected about where I was in life, I felt a sense of peace come over me, and I decided that should be the next step. Now that I was at peace with myself, I was in control of my own emotions. I had the ability to self-regulate and assess myself to determine what I needed. It felt amazing to not always focus on what other people needed. By going to therapy, I had learned to focus on me and my own experiences and feelings. It was a great feeling.

The last part of the pyramid I hadn't reached yet was joy. I put a star by it. Joy is different from happiness. It is an internal sense of peace and acceptance. When I reached joy, it would mean I accepted my past and was no longer controlled by it.

I could easily identify what I needed and be my own voice. Although I hadn't reached the last part yet, I had faith that, with God's help, it was on the horizon. I saw it manifesting a little with David. I was impressed by how I had ignored my negative thoughts and didn't change my plans to quit based on David's sad story and puppy dog face.

For the first time in my life, I felt free. Codependency had weighed me down, and I no longer wanted to help people. Helping people had brought me into a depression. I didn't know how to express my thoughts to people. I didn't know what to expect if I told people I couldn't support them, and that created my anxiety. I felt like my voice didn't matter to most people. What mattered was what I could do for them. I didn't get praise for being myself. I received praise for my accomplishments, so I created more opportunities for people to praise me by accomplishing more goals in life. I excelled in my career and education, but I didn't really want to.

Throughout my entire life, my goal was to be loved—real love without obligation. I dreamed of the day someone would love me, not because they felt they had to, but because they wanted to, because they saw the light, that I was just Taneshia, and they loved it. I longed for the day someone would see the beauty that is me without my accomplishments and love me.

I didn't have to wait for someone to come along and love me. I could love me. I could give myself that unconditional love I longed for, the love I had given everyone else. Everyone knew how amazing I was except me. I didn't want to believe it. Even when people told me I was, I assumed they were only saying it because they wanted to use me. I never thought people meant it when they said, "Taneshia, you're great" or "You're so sweet." Because if those things were true, why was I alone and crying myself to sleep almost every night?

Every day, I faithfully put my mask on. I played the role of a person who was happy, funny, and empathetic. All the while, I just wanted to be free. I longed to be free of helping other people, free to live my life how I wanted without worrying about everyone else. I learned that even the people who love you the most will hurt you. I found myself surrounded by people who were manipulating and emotionally abusing me; they consumed me. Everything was always about what they needed; they never were friends to me.

During my recovery, I spent many days by myself. I didn't know who to trust. Everyone seemed to want me to do something. Life felt hopeless. I found my refuge in God. I asked Him to help me find a group of people who would love and support me. I knew where I'd gone wrong in my life, and I was looking to God to be my saving grace.

God has the power to do anything. All power and honor belong to God. That is a rule I live by. Even in my weakest moments, I never doubted that God was able. I doubted if I was worthy and if He truly loved me. My thoughts were twisted during my depression, and my intrusive thoughts had a field day in my mind. My anxiety fueled my doubt and caused me to stumble in my faith.

Building my relationship with God helped me build a relationship with people who loved and cared about me. Once we let go of the relationships we think we need, God will send us the ones we deserve. When I let go of toxic, hurtful people in my life, God sent amazing people my way. To this day, I'm still shocked. I'm surrounded by people I prayed for, people who truly love me and want the best for my life. When I start feeling like episodes of depression are trying to form and my intrusive thoughts are entering my mind, they sit with me and pray. They text and call me. They spend time with me until I feel better. I didn't have that before. I no longer suffer in silence.

Maintaining a relationship with God was crucial in my life and a major coping strategy for me. Going out to a nightclub, starting a new intimate relationship, or getting drunk did nothing for my spirit. I wasn't aware that the self-care I needed was emotional and spiritual. I had lost my connection with God. That little girl who was excited about praying and amazed at how much God loved her was gone, but I had to get her back. I had to get back the spirit I had when I was a little girl.

Introducing me to God at four years old was the best thing my mother could have done for me. It opened a relationship that changed my life, and I knew it had the power to help me. God's love changed me. It was my resting place. When my mother was exhausted and couldn't be there for me and my dad didn't know how to be there for me, I had God. I may not have had a voice with people, but I always had one in prayer. My ultimate Father, my Creator, who listened to me go on and on and never told me to stop. I had a voice with Him. He listened to every word, every tear and loved me just as I was. When I was depressed, He reminded me that I was His child. When anxiety and negative thoughts came, He reminded me that I could do all things because of His love and His strength. I wasn't pouring His Word into me, and that's why I was suffering to sustain and survive.

Looking back on my life and episodes with anxiety and

depression, I thank God. I thank Him for every hardship that came my way. Had it not been for those tough times, I would still be trying to save the world and not myself. Self-care is bigger than activities we do for fun. It's about how we nurture and pour into our spirits, what we allow in our space and mind and how we honor and value ourselves daily.

Emotional self-care involves acknowledging and accepting our weaknesses and loving ourselves despite them, feeling free of having to dismiss our feelings. When we love ourselves, we honor our feelings and emotions and practice expressing ourselves in healthy ways. We know we are deserving of love, and we treat ourselves as such. We don't allow people to use us, and we set limits and boundaries to avoid feeling burnt out and depleted.

If you are struggling to learn how to take care of yourself, know that you are not alone. Never would I have thought being abandoned in a hotel room in Las Vegas would become my saving grace and ignite a journey to finding myself. I didn't know what self-love was, much less what it meant to practice loving myself. I was too busy loving everyone else, hoping that if I gave them what they needed, they would give me the validation and love I needed. I never thought loving myself was something I could do, and it would be enough. I didn't know how.

Every day, I am learning how, and it's an amazing journey. I love myself when I'm down and when I feel great. I speak up for myself. I can set a boundary with someone without guilt or shame. I don't concern myself with how other people feel. I allow people to feel and experience things without my input. I don't seek validation from others, nor do I desire it. I have the power to speak life into myself, and I practice it daily. I use

"I am" statements to encourage myself when I'm down. I can eliminate negative thoughts from my mind before they cause anxiety and depression.

When anxiety and depression have a voice in your head, life can feel challenging. You are not alone in how you feel. I have been there and have overcome. The power you have in yourself is what you need to sustain. Do not be afraid to seek professional help and take medication if needed. I want to warn you that professional help and medication can be life changing, but what you really need to overcome depression and anxiety is self-love. Love yourself enough to do the work to heal. Speak with those you feel have wronged and hurt you. Change your narrative, and break the negative patterns in your life. Stop blaming everyone else for the damage you have caused in your own life. Yes, people hurt you. We're all human, but we have control over who hurts us. We have control over who we allow into our minds and hearts. Don't allow people that mean you no good to take up residence in your life. You are worthy of everything you want and desire. You have a life full of peace and love waiting for you.

Just like I found mine, I know you will find yours, too.

Thank you for reading *When Depression
and Anxiety Have a Voice*
If you enjoyed this book, please leave an online review.

CONNECT WITH TANESHIA JOHNSON
Website: www.tjselfcare.com
Facebook: TJSelfcare
Instagram: @tjselfcare

Made in the USA
Columbia, SC
18 May 2020

97684724R00090